1,001
Ways to
SLOW DOWN

1,001 Ways to SLOW DOWN

A LITTLE BOOK OF EVERYDAY CALM

barbara ann kipfer

Illustrations by
Francesca Springolo

NATIONAL GEOGRAPHIC

Washington, D.C.

Since 1888, the National Geographic Society has funded more than 12,000 research, exploration, and preservation projects around the world. National Geographic Partners distributes a portion of the funds it receives from your purchase to National Geographic Society to support programs including the conservation of animals and their habitats.

National Geographic Partners
1145 17th Street NW
Washington, DC 20036-4688 USA

Become a member of National Geographic and activate your benefits today at natgeo.com/jointoday.

For information about special discounts for bulk purchases, please contact
National Geographic Books Special Sales: specialsales@natgeo.com

For rights or permissions inquiries, please contact National Geographic Books
Subsidiary Rights: bookrights@natgeo.com

ISBN: 978-1-4262-1779-1

Printed in China
17/RRDS/1

*No one needs this book more than I do,
and I dedicate this book to the people
who have had the most patience
with my driven nature: Paul Magoulas,
Kyle Kipfer, and Keir Magoulas. Thank you
also to my friend and colleague Bob Amsler,
whose technical skills help me produce
the best possible books.*

Introduction

My slow-down philosophy can be summed up in one word: "balance." It is about living at the speed that brings you the most joy and satisfaction.

In this second book in the 1,001 series, I offer 1,001 ways—both practical and spiritual—to relax, rethink, reorganize, and reimagine your life. I've also included my favorite inspirational quotes and lists of calming things to do to help you turn down the volume on the outside world and tune in to that quiet inside you.

Writing this book hit close to home. As its editor said to me, "You move at the speed of lightning!" I was always the first to finish my tests in school, I packed 200 moving boxes in less than a month, and I always finish projects ahead of deadlines. Because this is my nature, I have trouble slowing down and enjoying the processes. I have dedicated much of my life and spirituality to counteracting my natural impulse to push ahead quickly. Since sixth grade, I have been an ethnographer, making lists of the little things in life. If you don't slow down, you will miss them. Our happiness is tied to paying attention and being awake and aware in the moment. You can't do that at hyperspeed!

I now take great joy in moving slowly. I like to write books in longhand rather than on a computer. I wash the dishes by hand, except on Thanksgiving and Christmas. I use a regular toothbrush without batteries or a plug. I value a home-made meal, a well-written email without spelling mistakes, and leisurely walks where I remember what I see. Somewhere in the midst of these unrushed activities, I find delicious moments of calm.

My wish is for you to use this book of ideas and reminders to achieve more balance in your life and to take the time to appreciate every minute of every day.

1

Unplug.

2

Stop the busywork. Devote your time
to work that is satisfying.

3

Change your work hours to
accommodate your life.

4

Work from home one day a week.

5

Before you go to bed, pause to send good
thoughts to the people you love.

6

Practice being a flaneur (an idler or lounger).

7

Deliberately walk slowly. There is great pleasure to be had in ambling.

8

Spend hours in a coffee shop reading.

9

Whenever possible, abandon the hope of being somewhere at a specific time.

10

Calm leads to clarity; clarity leads to calm. It's cyclical.

11

Watch a flower slowly open its petals.

12

When you write, make time for revising
and improving your work.

13

Don't time your exercise.
Work out for a reasonable,
comfortable time and then stop.

14

Take time to be with nature.
Take time to be with people.
Take time to be with music.
Take time to be with children.

15

Instead of getting agitated when you are
stuck in traffic, think of this time as a pause—
a time when you cannot hurry.

16

When you have a lot to do, tackle one
thing at a time.

17

Do nothing upon waking up. Ask yourself,
"What is my intention for today?"
Pause occasionally throughout the day
to revisit your intention.

18

Slow down by several miles an hour
when driving. You will arrive just a few minutes
later and much more relaxed.

19

Imagine floating in a cloud you see in the sky.

20

Watch autumn leaves parachute slowly out of trees
and tumble gently across the landscape.

21

Every moment is a doorway to joy, meaning,
and purpose. The key is an unhurried mind.

22

Don't just shovel the snow, take time to play with it:
Roll snowballs, build a snowman, or make snow angels.

23

Picnic for breakfast, lunch, or dinner, and
slow down to the pace of nature.

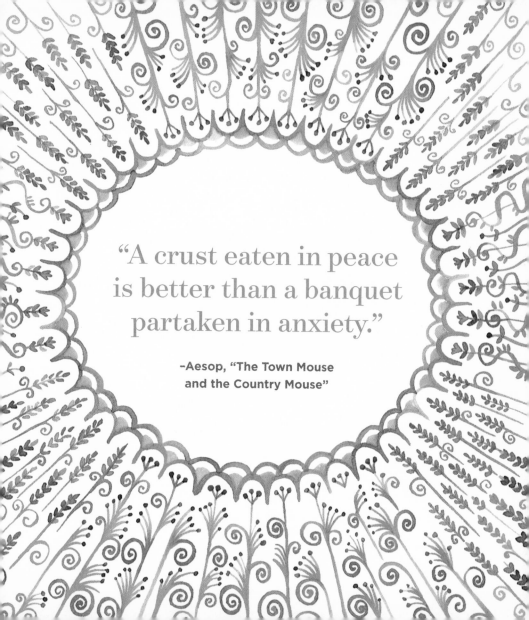

"A crust eaten in peace
is better than a banquet
partaken in anxiety."

–Aesop, "The Town Mouse
and the Country Mouse"

24

The world becomes a more magical place
as you let go of the constraints of time.

25

Consider a move to a smaller house.
It is a relief not to have to worry about
a big house and yard when the home
no longer fits your needs.

26

Create a jigsaw or word-search puzzle
and send it to a friend.

27

Make your trip home from work a relaxing
transition time by breathing and smiling.

28

In Italy there is the concept of *la passeggiata*—
a gentle evening stroll taken after dinner
and usually with family. End your day
with a calming family ritual.

29

Do not talk with your mouth full. Slow down,
clear your palate, and then talk.

30

If you feel panicky, make a conscious effort
to calm down. Tell yourself to stop panicking,
and then close your eyes and breathe slowly
and deeply. Feel yourself becoming more relaxed.
Notice your heartbeat slowing down.

31

Place the calming scent of lavender
in your bedroom.

32

If you are waiting for an important
phone call or email, view it as a time
to turn your focus to something else.
Worrying does not change the situation.

33

Accept whatever you are doing, even if
you'd rather be doing something else.

34

Speak with kindness.

35

If you inch closer to a stoplight, do you think the light will change more quickly?

36

Relax by closing your eyes and counting backward from 100.

37

Caress a smooth, rounded stone or prayer beads to focus the mind and calm anxiety.

38

Build rejuvenating breaks into your day.

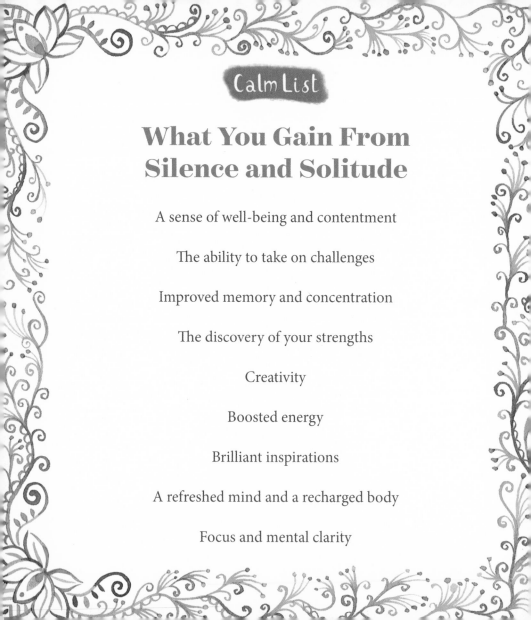

Calm List

What You Gain From Silence and Solitude

A sense of well-being and contentment

The ability to take on challenges

Improved memory and concentration

The discovery of your strengths

Creativity

Boosted energy

Brilliant inspirations

A refreshed mind and a recharged body

Focus and mental clarity

Greater self-control

Reduced anger

Improved communication and listening skills

Patience

Inner peace

Deeper sleep

The ability to respond instead of react

The easing of anxiety and depression

A quieter mind

Relaxation

Lowered stress levels

A stronger immune system

The ability to remove or ignore distractions

39

The only thing you have control over is
your mind. Teach yourself to let thoughts go
and clear your mind.

40

Avoid making some decisions today.

41

Dry your laundry on a clothesline,
where it can be buffeted by the breeze
and warmed by the sun.

42

Walk in a maze or labyrinth. With each step,
you'll feel lighter and more connected
to your inner voice.

43

Peace begins inside you.

44

A long wait will seem very short if you
are present and content.

45

Maybe you love the work you do, but the
structure of your work is not right for you.
Can you change your professional environment
or hours to suit your work style? Look for
the "sweet spot" in your working life.

46

Staying home can help you cut through
the noise and find fresh time and energy
to share with others.

47

Take slow, deep breaths while on the telephone,
in the car, or simply waiting.

48

Slow down and enjoy eating.

49

If your workplace is chronically noisy,
try wearing earplugs or noise-canceling
headphones to shut out sound.

50

Drawing 10 or fewer breaths per minute helps
the body relax and bolsters energy
and cognitive ability.

51

The next time you interrupt what you are
doing to check your phone, stop. We live in a
24/7 world based on immediacy. Do what you can
to slow this down to the speed of a happy life.

52

Spend the morning in bed watching
an old movie and being lazy.

53

Break hard or unpleasant news
to someone gently; don't rush.

54

Give yourself at least 30 minutes each
for lunch and dinner.

"Art has something to do with the achievement of stillness in the midst of chaos ... an arrest of attention in the midst of distraction."

–Saul Bellow

55

Park farther away from an entrance
and enjoy the walk.

56

Don't fill silences with words.
Relax and be aware.

57

Take time for long, thoughtful conversations
with interesting people.

58

In moments of rest after exercise or yoga,
absorb the benefits of your practice.

59

When you get to your office in the morning,
sit down and look out the window or at a wall.
Do not act. Do not talk. Just sit for
three whole minutes. This exercise can
start your day out right.

60

Philosophize.

61

Write with a fountain pen, experiencing the slow,
cutting drag of the nib against the paper grain.

62

Sit on the front porch and watch
your neighborhood at play.

63

Think of the music an iceberg makes as it melts:
the drip of water, the pop of air escaping,
the crack of the ice breaking apart.

64

Don't rush to the mailbox the minute
the postal worker walks or drives away.

65

Before turning the car key in the ignition—pause.

66

Support those who do slow work,
such as local farmers, local bakers,
and craft brewers.

Foods That Are Best When Cooked Slowly

Apple butter

Barbecue

Beef stew

Bolognese sauce

Cajun jambalaya

Chicken mole

Coq au vin

Corned beef and cabbage

Five-alarm chili

Homemade soup

Pork in all its forms: chops, loin, roasted, or pulled

67

Find a day where your only obligation
is to walk slowly through a meadow.

68

Turn off your mobile devices and put them
in a drawer for an hour—or a day.

69

Take power naps.

70

Immerse yourself in nature.

71

Try to enjoy the journey instead
of living in a habit of rushing.

72
Read calming quotations.

73
Look at beautiful photography.

74
When you practice meditation,
you will gravitate toward people
and situations that help you feel calm,
supported, and relaxed.

75
Let a vehicle cut in front of you on the roadway.

76
Try this affirmation: "I am happy just as I am.
I am peaceful with what is happening."

77

Seek refuge and restoration in the countryside.

78

Go for a swim.

79

Learn how to say no to excess commitments
and say yes to your well-being.

80

When you are in a meeting with
a colleague or colleagues, leave your phone
and computer at your desk.

81

Enjoy what you already have right in front of you.

82

When you complete a task, bring your
attention inward, close your eyes,
and breathe slowly and deeply 8 to 10 times
before you start your next task.

83

Finish the sentence, "If I had more time,
I would …" The next week, find the time.

84

When you take a nap, turn off anything
that will make noise.

85

Write in a journal. This is a helpful way
of checking in with where you are in life.

"Besides the noble art
of getting things done,
there is the nobler art
of leaving things undone ...
The wisdom of life consists
in the elimination
of nonessentials."

–Lin Yutang

86
Take the time to prepare.

87
Be swift to hear and slow to speak.

88
We go over and over what we have to do today,
what we did yesterday, or what must be
done tomorrow. The more you can let go
of this analytical thinking, the slower
your thoughts will flow.

89
Learn to live in a way in which you
have no enemies to struggle with
and no battles to win.

90

Make a pact with yourself not to answer
work calls or emails on the weekend.

91

Do not postpone goofing off
until Saturday or Sunday.

92

Use handheld garden tools instead
of gas-powered machines.

93

Learn how to procrastinate without
getting yourself in trouble.

94
Walk like a three-year-old exploring the world.

95
Take the time to always put your turn signal on when driving. It's the law.

96
Leave your desk for your lunch break.

97
Pick a route that takes twice the time to reach the exact same destination.

98
Zen and Taoist belief systems suggest that doing nothing may be a sign of wisdom, the highest good. The aim is to be in the present moment and fully aware.

99
Sway to quiet music with your eyes closed.

100
Really read your page-a-day calendar.

101
If something is worthy of only partial attention,
is it really worth doing?

102
The path to contentment is as close as
a long walk with someone you love.

103
When you are in the middle of chaos, be aware
that it will pass. Breathe and just accept it.

104

Routines like putting on and taking
off makeup are often carried out on autopilot.
Appreciate the artistry of applying it—and the fresh,
clean feeling you have after removing it.

105

Read one chapter per week of a very long novel.
Savor every word.

106

Ask your question and wait for an answer.

107

Wait for food to cool before eating it.

Slow Movies to Savor

2001: A Space Odyssey (1968)

Amélie (2001)

Barry Lyndon (1975)

Caché (2005)

Groundhog Day (1993)

It's a Wonderful Life (1946)

Life Is Beautiful (1997)

Midnight in Paris (2011)

A River Runs Through It (1992)

Shirley Valentine (1989)

Spring, Summer, Fall, Winter ... and Spring (2003)

The Straight Story (1999)

The Treasure of the Sierra Madre (1948)

108

When you climb into bed, close your eyes
and create a "news capsule" version of your day.
Run through the "headlines" from start to finish.
This will help you let go of the day's events
and fall asleep.

109

Take up one of the "lost arts," such as sewing,
rug braiding, or quilting.

110

Spend more time in the sun.

111

Write a real letter. Imagine the pleasure your
words will bring to the recipient.

112

Try to draw something you see each day.

113

Patience is accepting what is.

114

Practice yoga's 61-point relaxation exercise—
a gradual, systematic movement and release
from one point in the body to the next every one
or two breaths, relaxing each point.

115

Play spiritual music to soothe your soul.

116

When you are about to act on impulse,
take the time to ask if this action is really
in your best interest.

117

Divide housekeeping into stages or sections.
Allow plenty of time for each task.

118

When you are waiting on the phone with Muzak,
see it as a directive to pause and breathe.

119

Try yin yoga.

120

As you slow down, you will find that peace
and responsiveness will replace reactions.

121

Instead of acting on every distracting thought,
make a list of the ones you want to address later.

122

Master the art of focusing on one thing at a time.

123

Keep a stress diary to help you identify the causes
and patterns of stress symptoms. This can help
you make changes to reduce stress.

"For fast-acting relief,
try slowing down."

–Lily Tomlin

124

Direct your attention to the bottoms
of your feet and breathe.

125

Take lots of time for "being" instead
of always "doing."

126

Consider whether you can take time off
from a career to raise your children.

127

Walk into the welcome silence of your home
after a day filled with sound.

128

Take time to reflect on the true meaning
of each holiday that you observe.

129

Minimize clutter.

130

If you have a shed, see it as a retreat
or a canvas.

131

Find a place to be alone and dream.

132

Close your eyes and focus on your breath for as
long as you feel comfortable. Check the time
when you open your eyes. You may be surprised
at how much or how little time has passed.

133

Stop and smell the potpourri.

134

Choose an easy-care, five-minute hairdo that
is not affected much by weather changes.

135

Walk meditatively in circles,
without a destination.

136

When you allow yourself to be present
in the activity at hand, you may transcend
time altogether.

137

Children benefit from calm just as much
as their parents do.

Calm List

Times to Slow Down ... Quickly

Angry Moments
Take a few minutes to pause when
you are about to react.

Bedtime
Create a calming process, helping the
body and mind change modes
for a restful sleep.

Before Speaking
Ask yourself if what you are about to say
improves on silence.

Behind the Wheel
When driving, protect yourself and others by
remaining calm and obeying the law.

Celebrations
Slow the pace during holidays and special occasions
so you'll remember these good times later.

First Times
Go slowly when trying new things so you savor
what is happening.

On Stage
Before a performance or presentation, do breathing
exercises so you present your best self.

Sad Times
Don't rush to feel better. You need to heal.

Sick Days
Don't push yourself when you are sick, because your
body is demanding that you slow down.

When It Hurts
When you feel pain, stop. Going further could mean
a longer-lasting injury.

138

Be like a tree. Open your palms to the sky
and spread your arms like branches.

139

Be open and patient wherever you are.

140

Visit an art gallery at a slow time when you can
quietly contemplate works of art.

141

If you have a competitive, goal-driven job,
balance it with a noncompetitive pastime,
such as yoga or painting.

142

Consider going to work early or staying late
to work without interruption.

143

On a beautiful day, hold a work meeting outside.

144

Look for the good in this moment.

145

Resist pressure from others to get things done
sooner than you really need to.

146

At a conference or event where you have
to be "on," create pockets of time to be alone.

147

Chew food slowly.

148
Get enough sleep before a long drive.

149
Hear the wind murmuring, the leaves rustling,
the birds flapping their wings—
and yourself quietly breathing.

150
Pretend that you are a stick drifting along
a quiet, lazy stream on a sunny day.

151
Water your lawn slowly and deeply.
This is more effective than shorter,
more frequent dousings.

152

Go on a gratitude walk. Appreciate the great, pleasing, beautiful, funny details in each and every thing.

153

Watch every action, every thought, every desire—even the smallest gestures. The more watchful you are, the more calm you can become.

154

Realize that what is important to you right now will likely not be important to you in a year.

155

Relax your tongue and jaw, and even touch your lips.

"He bites his tongue who speaks in haste."

–Turkish proverb

156

Break a long-distance walk
into bite-size pieces.

157

Throw a casual dinner party with great
wine and conversation.

158

Take a school-day approach to your time:
Make equally predictable periods
for work, play, and rest.

159

Hang a stained-glass decoration in
a sunny window. Enjoy the relaxing
play of light in the room.

160

Imagine timelessness—a pause
in the spinning of the world.

161

Buy, store, cook, and consume your
food at a relaxed pace.

162

Take a "brain break" of 10 minutes every hour.

163

Take your pulse, counting to four.
Relax, breathe, and try to gain a longer
pause between each pulse, slowing
and soothing your heart.

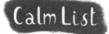
Calm List

Relaxing Hobbies to Try

Doodling in an art journal

Bird-watching

Blogging

Building a boat

Writing stories

Flying a kite

Composing or playing music

Needlepoint, cross-stitch, embroidery, or weaving

Tinkering with machines

Exploring yoga in its many forms

Singing to your heart's content

164
A sense of humor is enormously
helpful in times of stress.

165
Knitting is so slow that one sees the beauty
inherent in every tiny stitch.

166
There is nothing wrong with declining
to attend a party.

167
Choose quality over quantity in your relationships.

168
At day's end, drop all anxieties and allow yourself
to sink into the peaceful pool of your quiet mind.

169

Study the rock cycle—specifically
metamorphic rock flowing extremely slowly,
twisting the layers within.

170

Stop regularly during a long car journey
to stretch, eat and drink, and relax.

171

Listen to your body and respect its limits;
push ahead slowly.

172

Remember that unstructured play is important
for kids and grown-ups.

173
Your peace of mind lies not in
your individual circumstances, but in how
you respond to them.

174
Practice kindness.

175
Save part of a good restaurant meal
for lunch the next day.

176
Partake in or appreciate the slow,
disciplined work of vineyards, of archaeology,
of lexicography, of climbing mountains,
of meditation.

177

Enjoy a full day at a state fair.

178

Allow at least as much time for eating
mindfully as the time required
to prepare the meal.

179

After you have learned to simply "be"
in the slow motion of stillness, learn how
to simply "be" in the midst of great action.

180

Spending money to solve a problem has become
a quick fix in itself. The truth is, "this too
shall pass"—and perhaps you should let it.

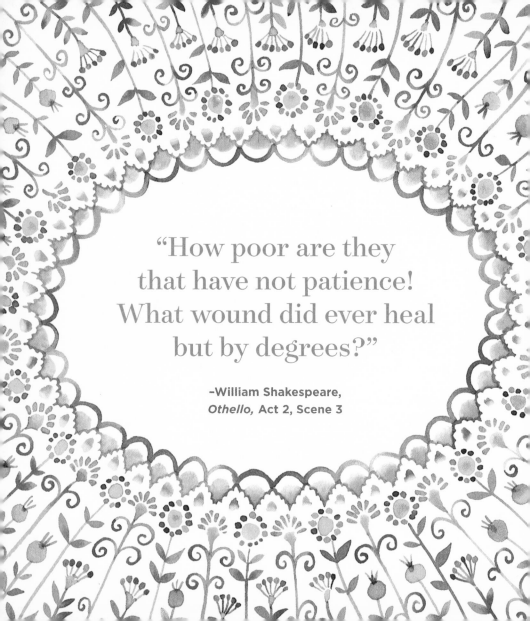

"How poor are they
that have not patience!
What wound did ever heal
but by degrees?"

–William Shakespeare,
Othello, Act 2, Scene 3

181

Observe snow as it falls, transforming
the landscape.

182

Let the very act of reading be peaceful.

183

Busyness is a choice.

184

Before you focus on the next item on your
to-do list, pause to feel a sense of accomplishment
for completing prior tasks on the list.

185

Go to bed when you are tired.

186

Nervousness about situations where you
feel a loss of control is normal. Slow your mind
and you will reduce your anxiety.

187

Relax about money. If you do work you enjoy,
the money you need will come.

188

Weed the garden by hand.

189

Listen to the sounds of silence.

190

Spend a day each week in natural time,
avoiding clocks, and doing things
when they feel right.

191

Choose to be patient when construction
vehicles are slowing traffic.

192

All of us have moments when we forget
time completely. It is in those moments
that we experience happiness.

193

Join a get-rich-slowly scheme.

194

When you get a new gadget, take the time
to get to know it properly. This saves time
in problem-solving later.

195

Take a break from it all and glide.

196

Remain seated until the airplane is at the gate
and the seat belt sign is turned off.

197

Speak from the heart.

198

Listen deeply.

199
Be compassionate and respectful.

200
A silent hike through nature is a form
of meditation.

201
Set aside a time for reflection.

202
Sense the ever changing waves around you,
breathe, and relax.

203
No matter what happens, remember
you are "home."

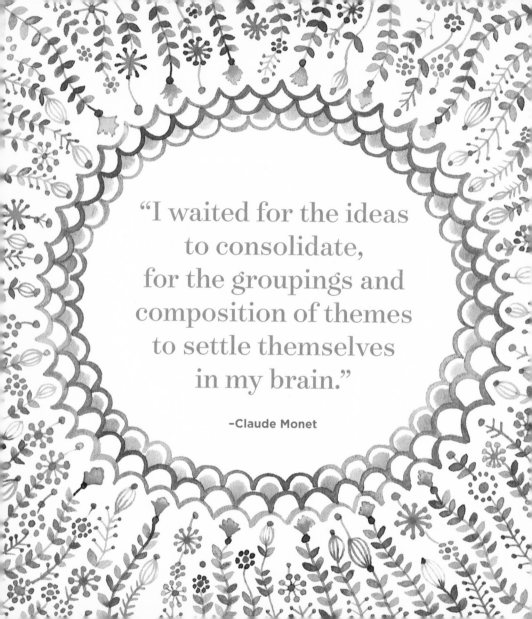

"I waited for the ideas
to consolidate,
for the groupings and
composition of themes
to settle themselves
in my brain."

–Claude Monet

204

In moments when you feel most adrift
and confused, silence offers a sanctuary
of renewal.

205

Discover the quiet delight of snowshoeing.

206

Let the ketchup come out of the bottle
at its own speed.

207

We play a lot of games in everyday life: picking the
fastest checkout line, taking off at a green light,
or timing a commute. Recognize when you are
involved in one of these "secret" competitions.
These areas may be ripe for slowing down.

208
The essence of mindfulness is to make
every moment your own.

209
In almost every culture, the garden is
a place to rest and ruminate.

210
Take advantage of the easy chairs
in a bookstore or library.

211
Studying your family's genealogy is slow going,
but the rewards are timeless.

212
Many people dread what they might have
to face in the absence of busyness.

213

Walk until your head is quiet.

214

Some people are boring, and you are not
obligated to spend time listening to them.

215

Be accommodating. Don't forget where your
preferences lie, but remain spacious
and relaxed when they are not met.

216

Learning how to "be" is a one-minute practice
that can be done anywhere at any time.
Breathe deep breaths. Then expand your attention
to the body and feel it as it is. Done regularly,
this simple practice becomes ingrained
and can be drawn on in difficult moments.

217

If you are oriented to the present moment,
you will need very few activities to feel a sense
of satisfaction with your life and experiences.

218

Travel across a state or country by rail.

219

Fishing is meditation. If you happen
to catch a fish—bonus!

220

Savor that movie you always wanted to see.

221

Go on a media fast and see if your life
feels different.

Calm List

Handwritten Letters to Send

To the president of the United States

To a friend, inviting them to do an exciting new activity

To yourself—a letter to read in the future

To someone you are thankful for

To someone who has impacted your life

To ask forgiveness

To restore a relationship

To be opened in the event of your death

To your great-great grandchild

To your partner—a love letter

To a "visual" person—art mail

To make someone's day

222

Go bird-watching. Observe the magic of flight
and the diversity of the animal world.

223

Instead of barking out directions
to family members, make lists for them.
This gives the receivers more autonomy in
fitting the tasks into their schedules.

224

Take time to hug someone every day.

225

Learn the art of wine tasting.

226

Play a game with a toddler.

227

Walking can teach you about your body's
built-in natural pace.

228

Sit back, relax, and be the designated listener.
It takes true concentration to follow another's words.

229

Observe the slow chiseling of water on rock.

230

Do away with all the things you do
only to impress people.

231

Reread an email before sending it
to make sure the tone is positive
and the spelling is correct.

232

Hurrying to find happiness outside yourself
makes as much sense as searching where
you've never been for something you lost.

233

Being still and open in silence and solitude helps
you return to that sense of childlike wonder.

234

Stroll to a meeting instead of racing.

235

Remember, life is funny.

236

Don't spend another minute looking for praise.

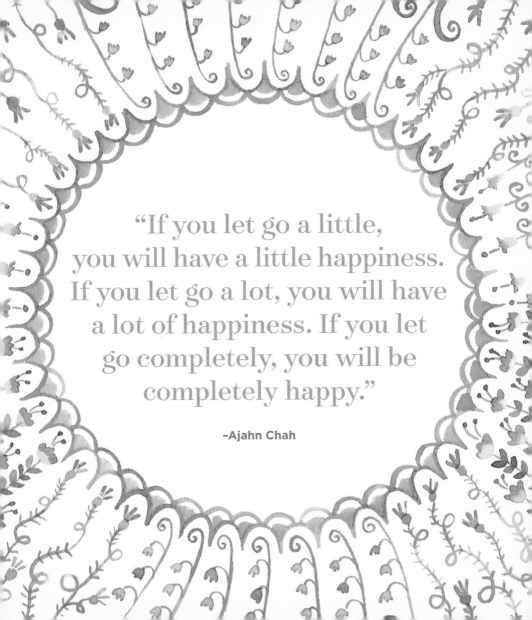

"If you let go a little,
you will have a little happiness.
If you let go a lot, you will have
a lot of happiness. If you let
go completely, you will be
completely happy."

–Ajahn Chah

237

Contemplate what is really important to you
in the long run.

238

When things go wrong, try to relax by
remembering that nothing is of lasting significance.
Everything will disappear, including you.

239

Read the last word on the last page
of an exquisite book, then do nothing but
stare out the window and let it linger.

240

Set aside time for extended silent periods
and retreats throughout the year
to renew your spirit.

241

Cross out everything on your to-do list
that is not actually necessary or beneficial.

242

At a hotel, unpack a snack, sprawl out
on the bed, and listen to the quiet.

243

Read a philosophy book with prose
so dense and intriguing that it must be
read extremely slowly.

244

Stand every 20 minutes to break up sitting time.

245

Think before speaking to avoid saying
unkind words you don't mean.

Calm List

Sights to Stop and Gaze At

Sunrises

Rainbows

The first snow of the year

Meteor showers

A baby sleeping

Your lover sleeping

Your pet sleeping

Aurora borealis

Clouds passing by

A lit candle

Flowers

A favorite painting

Lightning storms

A blazing fireplace

Life under a rock

City lights from a rooftop

Mountains through an airplane window

Crashing waves

The underside of a waterfall

A desert sky

A deep crevasse

Marine life underwater

An eclipse

Tides ebbing and flowing

Sunsets

246

If you went too far in exercising yesterday,
take a break today.

247

Watch cartoons on Saturday morning.

248

Spend a day each month in solitude.

249

Meditation works like a snow globe:
It helps the flaky stuff in your mind settle down
so you can see more clearly.

250

Make sure you have a great deck chair
for naps, basking, and relaxing.

251

Did you know that boredom is a
modern invention? The word came into use
only in the 1850s. Instead of considering
boredom onerous, try to view it as
an intense experience of time.

252

Look for the color blue in your surroundings.
Some say it causes the body to produce chemicals
that relax the nervous system.

253

It is on your busiest days that the effects
of some quiet time are the greatest.

254

Stare at a beautiful image instead
of reading an article.

255
Talk to your plants.

256
Retrain in the lost art of doing nothing.

257
Enjoy an old-fashioned candy that takes
a long time to eat, such as a Slo Poke,
sugar buttons, or taffy.

258
Change the next moment by breaking a pattern
and doing something differently.

259
See the knife actually break the skin
of a fruit or vegetable as you start to cut it.
That is mindfulness.

260

Be strong enough to let go and
patient enough to wait.

261

Read poetry.

262

Listen to a recording of nature sounds
at bedtime.

263

You learn to slow down by consciously
trying to slow down.

264

Peruse an old-fashioned print encyclopedia.

265
Smell the fresh-cut grass.

266
Be open to not knowing.

267
People who cut their work hours take
a smaller financial hit than you might expect.
Less time on the job may mean spending less
on transportation, parking, childcare,
and other expenses.

268
Choose how you spend your time.

269
Take up a slow form of exercise,
such as yoga or weight lifting.

270

Allow the character of a place
or person to sink in slowly.

271

Don't pull every weed. Let them coexist
with flowers and plants.

272

The way to open a package may become
clearer if you first take time to think about it.

273

Write in longhand.

274

Many martial arts have lightning-fast kicks
and punches, but participants maintain
a core of stillness and focus.

275

Stop criticizing the too-slow waiter.

276

An immediate response is necessary
in very few situations.

277

You can only see living things grow if you wait.

278

If there is a disagreement, tell someone
how you feel and listen to his or her point
of view. Then calmly decide what to do.

279

Speak softly and warmly.
This will slow down your speech.

"How beautiful it is
to do nothing,
and then to rest
afterward."

–Spanish proverb

280
Skip a workout if you need something else more, such as meditation.

281
Do not feel pressured to have answers and opinions about everything.

282
Tap into your natural rhythms to be at your most productive when it counts.

283
Watch classic movies that move at a slower pace than today's films.

284
Savor a soup you made from scratch.

285

Think of yourself as a cat, completely relaxed in front of a warm fire.

286

Give yourself permission to drop or delegate some commitments.

287

Enjoy the constantly changing sculpture of a slow-burning candle.

288

You are probably at your most creative when the pressure is off and ideas can simmer on the back burner.

289
Clear space in your schedule for rest,
daydreaming, and serendipity.

290
Open presents slowly and dramatically.

291
Plan large projects to avoid a mad dash
to make a deadline.

292
Consciously slow your talking.

293
Instead of pushing away life's obstacles,
think of ways to work around
or through them.

294

What difference would it make in your life
to renounce hurrying for one week—
or even one day?

295

Read about Epicureanism and Epicurus,
who promoted emotional calm
and intellectual pleasures.

296

Enjoy the slow-motion feeling of walking
on a beach as the sand tugs at your feet.

297

Come up with personalized ways
to simplify your life.

Calm List

Slow Sports to Enjoy

Archery

Baseball

Bocce

Bowling

Canoeing

Cricket

Curling

Fishing

Golf

Hiking

Horseshoes

Paddleboarding

298

There is nothing to rush off to that can offer you anything more than this moment.

299

When you stumble on an unfamiliar word or concept, take the time to look it up and learn.

300

You may be shocked by the difference it makes when you relax your dependence on clock time.

301

Saving money is a slow process that has many benefits.

302

Slow scenes to imagine: water trickling
in a fountain, the calm after a storm, hot-air
balloons drifting, a desert island.

303

Doing two things at once often means
doing both things not very well.

304

Focus on every movement while falling asleep.
Breathe consciously.

305

When you are waiting in a long line,
make a new friend or just enjoy
the action around you.

306

Come home and rest your head
on an old, familiar pillow.

307

Browse, putter, and dawdle.

308

If you listen in stillness, you will find
the wisdom you need.

309

Have a detox or fasting day each month.

310

Take up slow activities, such as drawing,
refinishing furniture, sewing, or writing.

311

Light a candle at the dining table during meals.

312

Life is too short to be busy all the time.

313

Have a long lunch with a good friend.

314

When you wake from a dream,
write down all the details in a notebook.
What are your dreams trying to tell you?

315

It is important to realize you cannot
absorb all of the information out there,
so choose selectively what you take in.

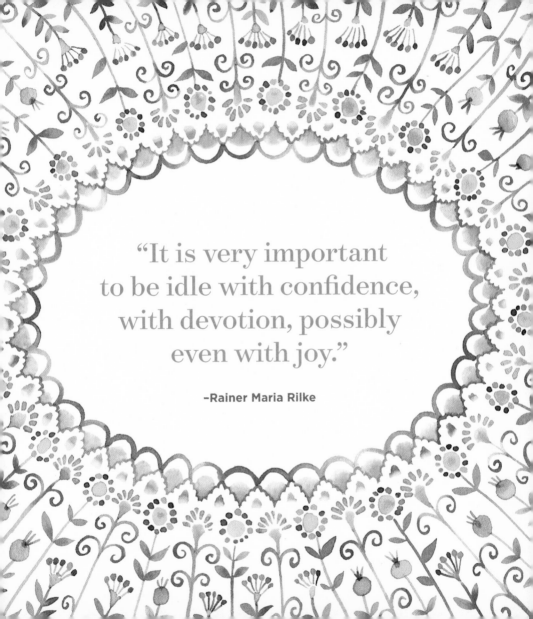

"It is very important
to be idle with confidence,
with devotion, possibly
even with joy."

–Rainer Maria Rilke

316
Notice your need for control,
whether over people, politics, your body,
your mind, your past, your future,
or even the weather.

317
Sharpen a pencil the old-fashioned way,
with a knife or sandpaper.

318
Drive the speed limit.

319
Stillness and silence can become
a radical act of courage.

320

Everything you need is right here, right now.

321

Make a Zen garden and meditate on the patterns created.

322

Write a thank-you note on paper and send it via snail mail.

323

Install a porch swing for a slow, lazy summer day.

324
Flaxseed eye pillows can help
relieve tension.

325
Make time to settle any quarrel
before bedtime.

326
Be patient: In time, even an egg will walk.

327
Watch the evening shadows
creep across a room.

328
Plant a tree.

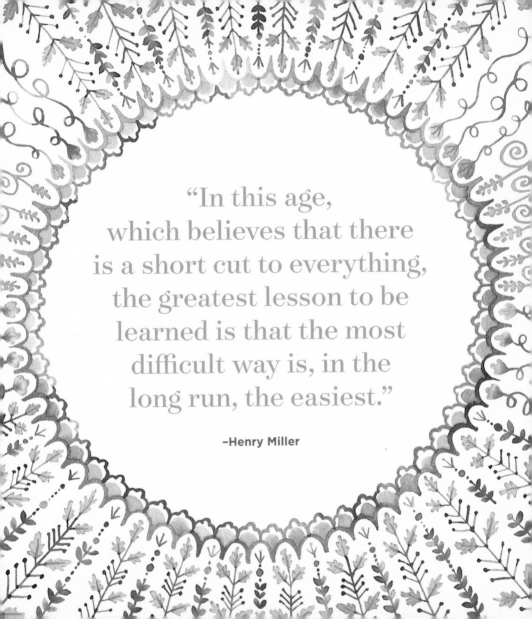

"In this age,
which believes that there
is a short cut to everything,
the greatest lesson to be
learned is that the most
difficult way is, in the
long run, the easiest."

–Henry Miller

329

Let the sun's rays gently warm you.

330

Pregnancy—the most important wait—
cannot be hurried.

331

Create places you can go in your mind
and heart to experience peace and quiet.

332

Take time to find the silver lining in each cloud.
Positivity breeds relaxation.

333

Ask for a postponement, deferral, or reprieve
when you really need it.

334

When you are home alone, take the time
to relax and indulge a little.

335

A nap is one of the easiest and most
satisfying ways to slow down.

336

Watch for someone who is not
in a hurry on a city street.

337

Use your entire vacation allotment each year.

338

Sow seeds and reconnect with the earth.

339

Doing nothing is not the same
as laziness or passivity.

340

Accumulate a new wardrobe slowly,
one piece per season or month.

341

Things that slow us down become the enemy.
This can turn into road rage, air rage, office rage,
or relationship rage. Stop the rage machine.

342

Each time you vacuum or iron, you can pretend
that you are sweeping or pressing away
your worldly attachments. Let them go
with the dust, dirt, and wrinkles.

343

In quiet moments, you will be pleasantly
surprised by your inspirations and insights.

344

By slowing down to the present moment,
you will be far more prepared for
the unexpected and for change.

345

Take a break to wash your face, eat a cookie,
smell something great, stretch, lie down,
or play with a pet.

346

If you have a fireplace, use it.

Calm List

Meditations to Try

Breathe
Take slow, deep breaths. Your desire to get moving
will relax into the moment.

Calm Yourself
Choose to do something that relaxes you:
Draw, listen to music, or research something
you are curious about.

Exercise
Yoga, tai chi, martial arts, running, bicycling,
and walking can be "moving meditation."

Focus
Pay attention to the way you move and do a simple task.
Become aware of all the parts of the process.

Memorize a Quote
Repeat it to yourself as a comforting technique.

Move Mindfully
Attempt to do a routine activity in slow motion.

Pause
Take a time-out whenever you are feeling
anxious or nervous.

Sit and Watch
Put your hands in your lap and simply look
around you. Close your eyes for a moment.

Stay in the Present
Focus on your breathing. When your mind
wanders from the breath to the past or future,
return your focus to the breath.
Practicing this basic meditation will bring
you great benefits over time.

Use Stoplights as Reminders
Notice if you wish to drive forward. This awareness
can help in other situations where you want
things to change.

347
Be unreachable for part of the day.

348
Read a long, old-fashioned fairy tale to a child.

349
Walk through the powerful silence of a forest embraced by its stillness.

350
Write down things you do not want to forget.

351
Take your time deciding whose advice to act on.

352

Spending less time watching television
or surfing the Internet may give you more time
to do the things you want to do.

353

Hike up hills.

354

Enjoy breaks in the clouds by observing the
shards of light that illuminate the ground.

355

Sit in a quiet place and silently empty your mind.

356

When lying in bed with your partner,
stay a little longer. Snuggle and feel the love.

357

Adopt *sprezzatura*, an easeful manner
of conducting oneself and doing things simply
and without concerted effort.

358

Meet friends at a restaurant rather than pressuring
yourself to put on a dinner party.

359

Don't catch the express bus.
Take the local and watch the people
come and go.

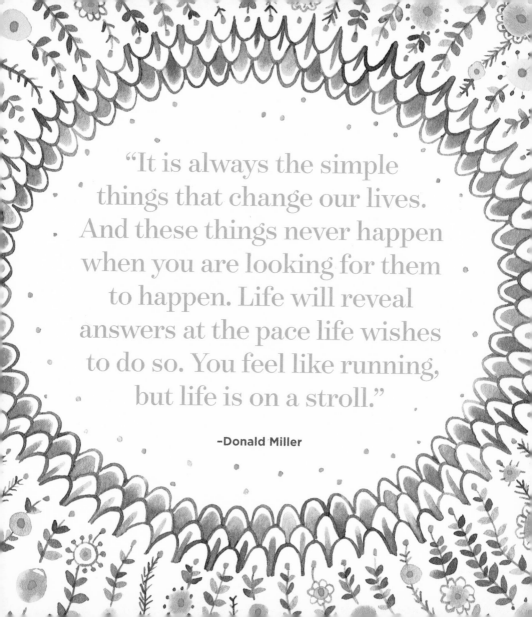

"It is always the simple things that change our lives. And these things never happen when you are looking for them to happen. Life will reveal answers at the pace life wishes to do so. You feel like running, but life is on a stroll."

–Donald Miller

360

Grasp the fragile instinct behind
a moment of hesitation.

361

Watch a river flow. The interplay
of the wind, temperature, and sun makes
for an infinitely changing scene.

362

Take children to farms to learn where
their meals come from.

363

Pausing means you are moving out
of thinking and doing, and into being.

364

Instead of guzzling down a beverage
(especially alcoholic), sip and savor the drink.

365

Play hooky and catch a movie matinee.

366

Ask yourself if the most difficult things
in your life are meant to be.

367

Join a book club whose members savor
the process of reading.

368

We all thirst for freedom and inner peace.
Silence is the medium for their discovery.

369

Sign up for an art course that involves
no rush, deadlines, or competition.

370

Relax in water. Rest in its simplicity
and buoyancy.

371

Scavenge used and rare bookstores.
Treasures await.

372

Visualize an ice cube melting
into hot coffee.

373

At the end of the workday, be satisfied
with doing one less thing.

374

It takes courage to slow down
and step out of the fray.

375

Enjoy a leisurely outdoor dinner
under the stars.

Calm List

Vacations to Help You Chill Out

Archaeological dig

Backpacking

Bicycle tour

Canoe and camping trip

Cross-country road trip

Cruise on an ocean liner

Glamping

Island getaway

Meditation retreat

Riverboat cruise

Scenic walking tour

376

Keep a list of words that interest you and look up their etymologies (word histories).

377

Next time you are craving an unhealthy food, set a timer for 20 minutes. When the timer goes off, check to see if you still want that food. Slowing down your urge helps you make a more mindful decision.

378

Notice any awkwardness or unnecessary effort when you sit or stand? Slowing down may make you more graceful.

379

You can use your mind to watch your mind—a uniquely human ability.

380

Try a calming tea blend with ginger,
green tea, licorice, or peppermint.

381

Sit outside and marvel at the slow climb of the sun,
the glacial travel of the shadows, the drift of a cloud.

382

Lie in a field among plants. See things from
their slow-growing perspective.

383

Lie down and imagine you are
at the edge of the sea on a beach.
Gentle waves move around your body
as you float in shallow water, gliding up
and down. Relax in profound calm.

384

Forget the GPS. Learn how to navigate
with a map and compass.

385

Spend less time on any relationship in which
you feel like Charlie Brown trying to kick
the football that Lucy is going to pull away.

386

Wander around in old churches.

387

Take the time to train your dog.
Your life (and your relationship with
your neighbors) will be easier as a result.

388
Remember that all habits are acquired slowly.

389
We tend to be most productive and happy
when we are moving at our natural pace.

390
Give yourself a choice between
a blind reaction and a creative,
considered response.

391
Set up a family night that does not
involve electronics.

392
Lie in a hammock.

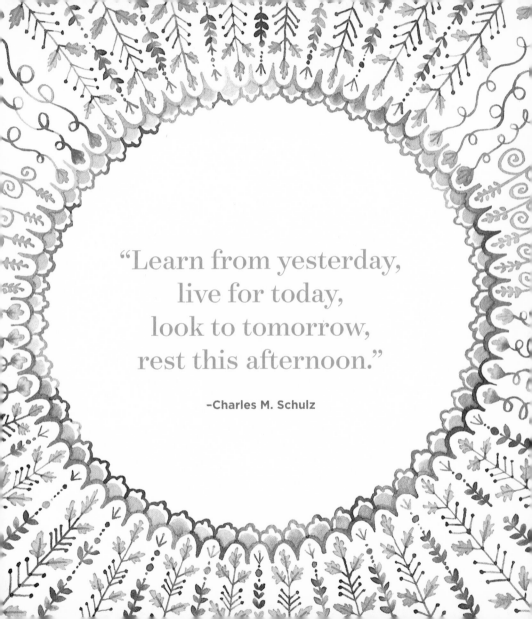

"Learn from yesterday,
live for today,
look to tomorrow,
rest this afternoon."

–Charles M. Schulz

393
Make a playlist of the most soothing pieces
of music you have.

394
The healing stillness of a quiet mind
nourishes every aspect of your life.

395
Cooking is a wonderful way to unwind.

396
Take the time to nurture your relationships.

397
Be like an island that no flood can engulf.

398
Observe yellow traffic lights; they are there for a good reason.

399
Times to enter silence and solitude present themselves every day. You just have to look for them.

400
Self-confidence helps you slow down because it reduces anxiety about everyday encounters.

401
Go on a real date with your partner.

402
Get lost in a library, often.

403
Devote much of your free time
to your curiosity.

404
Appreciate what you have already
achieved in life.

405
Read long, slow, calming, classic books.

406
Wait up for someone who had
a big evening out.

407

Make sure every kiss lasts at least
three seconds.

408

Watch a spider spinning its web.

409

Instead of succumbing to fast food, master
a simple meal that can be prepared
when you have less time to cook.

410

In the end, do you think you'll wish you had
worked harder and kept a cleaner house or that
you had spent more time relaxing, being with
loved ones, and enjoying nature?

Calm List

Activities That Are More Fun in Slow Motion

Cooking

Dinner date with your partner

Dog walking

Drinking hot chocolate

Eating

Gardening

Getting dressed

Kissing

Lovemaking

People-watching

Reading

Sketching

411

Sleep in!

412

When you take a morning walk,
pay attention to all the manifestations
of nature and its daily miracles.

413

Remember that only a quiet and
receptive mind can learn.

414

Work expands to fill the time available.

415

Instead of rushing to kill a bug, try to catch it
and release it outside. A lot of insects serve
a useful purpose. Put them back
where they belong and let them be.

416

Float in a pool, lake, or sea. Enjoy the motion
of the water and waves.

417

Congratulate yourself every time you reduce
your anger and control your reactions.

418

Bask in the enjoyment of a completed project.
Savor the success.

419

Turn off your email for short intervals
or set it to notify you only three times
per workday.

420

When you are using a product, anything
from a powder compact to a hiking stick,
think about the process and all the
people involved in creating that item.

421

Watch complete sunsets, from before dusk
until the sun disappears.

422

Let things be pleasant without grasping after them.
Let things be unpleasant without avoiding them.
Let things be neutral without trying to change
them to being pleasant. These are precepts
to follow in being happy with life.

423

Before you get out of bed each morning,
take five minutes to listen, see, smell,
breathe, observe.

424

Take mini-breaks at work. Close your eyes,
take deep breaths, or get up and stretch.

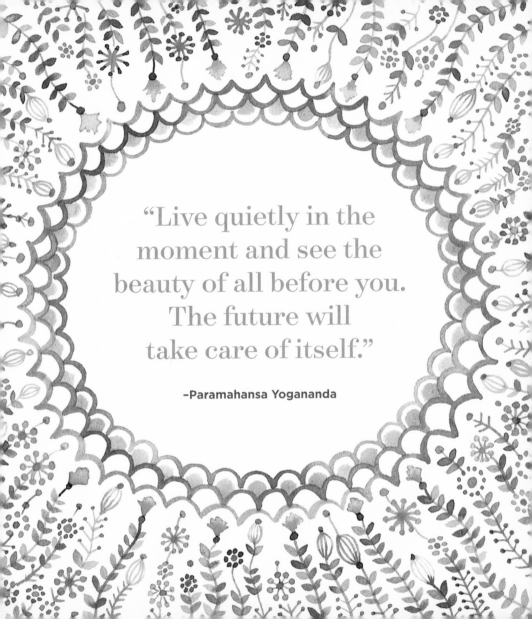

"Live quietly in the moment and see the beauty of all before you. The future will take care of itself."

–Paramahansa Yogananda

425

The remedy for anger is delay. The remedy
for a short temper is a long walk. The remedy
for any trouble is patience.

426

A softer, less frantic, simpler existence
is there for each of us. It starts by
slowing down and paying attention.

427

If you admit that you do not know something,
you will open the way to insight and an answer.

428

Choose a book to ruminate on. Step into
the story and try on the author or character's
realizations as your own.

429

Look up words in a printed dictionary.

430

Constantly reliving past events only
complicates your life. Take a moment
to think of something positive that came out
of the experience and then move on.

431

As you step back from the intensity of your
expectations and demands on life, you may be
surprised to discover that each moment holds
everything needed to find deep peace
and contentment.

432

You learn to slow down from the inside out.

433

Roast meat on a slow-turning spit.

434

If you buy something that has to be assembled,
take your time, read the instructions,
and it will turn out fine.

435

Join an outdoor tai chi or yoga group.

436

Your quality of life is created within;
it is not imposed by outside forces.

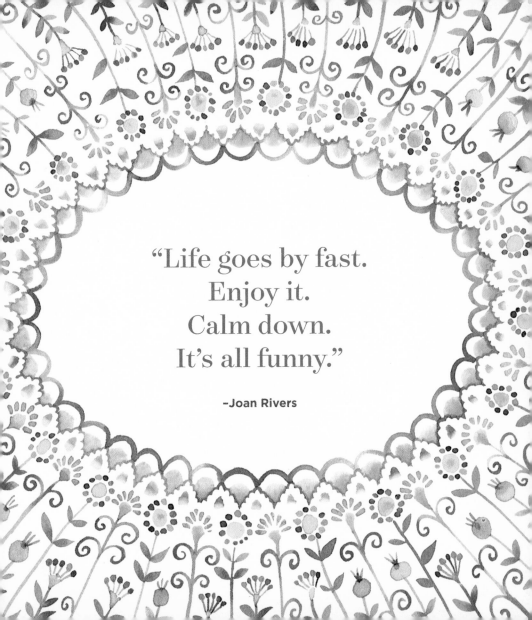

"Life goes by fast.
Enjoy it.
Calm down.
It's all funny."

–Joan Rivers

437

On separate sticky notes, write Breathe,
Pause, Laugh, Think. Post them in places
where you might need them.

438

Lie down and, with each out-breath,
sink deeper and deeper into the surface
you are lying on, letting go of any tension
or worry. Send love and compassion
to your whole body.

439

Let people know when you are running late.
Consideration takes time but it's worth it.

440

On an airplane trip, don't open a laptop,
read a novel, or watch a movie.

441

Quit trying so hard.

442

Slowly traverse a shoreline, stopping to
appraise shells and pebbles.

443

Spend a night or two in a hotel. Savor the break
from the routine of daily life.

Take the Time to Be Organized

Avoid Eleventh-Hour Completions
Whether it's a school paper or a work project, it is better to plan ahead and work gradually toward the goal.

De-clutter
Choose what you want to keep, and get rid of the rest.

Do One Thing at a Time
Letting go is more important than adding. If you cannot let something go, it is either an attachment to the past or a fear of the future.

Focus on What's Important
Happiness is about experiences that are savored.

Have Less Stuff
If you own a cow, the cow also owns you.

Keep Track of Personal Information

Knowing where your financial and personal information is—and protecting it—saves time and brings much peace of mind.

Make Shopping Lists

They help you buy what you need and avoid impulse purchases.

Organize Your Space

Find a good place for each thing and keep each thing in its place: grocery coupons in the kitchen, instructions for the new TV in the TV room, bill-paying items in the same drawer together.

Prioritize

Write down three tasks that need to be done today. Things fall into place once you've picked a direction.

Simplify Your Mind

Cut back on the amount of negative information and images you let penetrate your mind.

444

Remember how quickly time passes. It will
add meaning to every moment.

445

Between one thought and the next is a tiny gap
when the mind is at peace. Extending that gap
is the secret of an unhurried mind.

446

People who slow down manage to be on time
without arriving feeling hurried.

447

Keep a plant on your desk and take
good care of it.

448
Look at the leaves on the trees.

449
Use chopsticks to avoid eating too quickly.

450
In a restaurant, wait for your server to
come around with the menu or meal.
Do not call out for them or wave them over.

451
Self-control relaxes you because it
removes stress and enables you to conserve
willpower for important challenges.

452

Slow down getting on and off a highway.

453

Be slow to act on the first thought
that comes to mind.

454

Choose a day you can have all to yourself
for a personal retreat.

455

Cut down on processed fast foods.

456

Unplug as many devices as you can
when you are not using them.

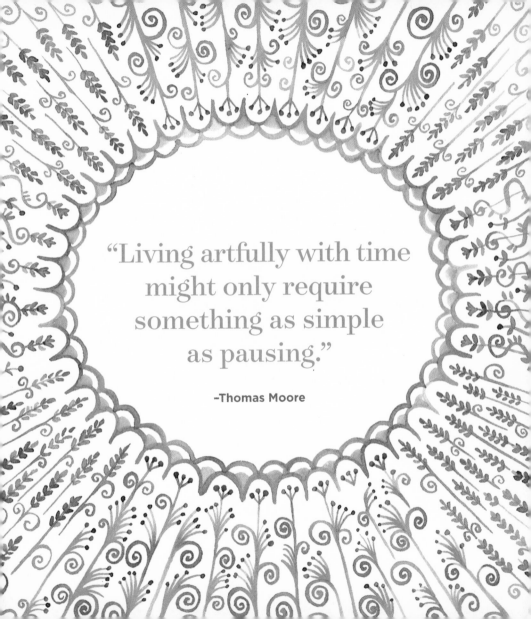

"Living artfully with time
might only require
something as simple
as pausing."

–Thomas Moore

457

Shift to geological time. Be a mountain range,
moving a millimeter at a time.

458

Most people's idea of the perfect holiday
consists of a leisurely time spent with family
and friends. Are there ways to make that happen
even when it's not a holiday?

459

Do not automatically turn on the radio
in your car or the television at home.

460

Breathe deeply before you speak.

461

Schedule waiting periods that force you
to linger in the present tense.

462

Simply notice your thoughts and let them go.
Your feelings of urgency will drop away.

463

Really take your coffee break.

464

The art of mindful living requires a lifetime
of gentle and determined effort.

465

Change what you can and don't worry
about the rest.

466

Appreciate children absorbed in quiet play.

467

When your mind is calm, your entire life
will seem more calm.

468

Art therapy can serve as the artistic equivalent
of a long, hot bath.

Calm List

Books to Take Your Time Reading

Anna Karenina (Leo Tolstoy)

C (Tom McCarthy)

Gilead (Marilynne Robinson)

The Goldfinch (Donna Tartt)

Harry Potter and the Deathly Hallows (J. K. Rowling)

Infinite Jest (David Foster Wallace)

In Search of Lost Time (Marcel Proust)

Moby-Dick (Herman Melville)

The Odyssey (Homer)

The Old Man and the Sea (Ernest Hemingway)

Song of Myself (Walt Whitman)

Ulysses (James Joyce)

469

Save news to tell people when you see them,
rather than texting or sharing via social media.

470

Freeze homemade dishes that can be easily defrosted
when time is tight, instead of ordering takeout.

471

Take the stairs instead of the elevator.

472

Gardening is soothing for the soul.

473

Appreciate the time you have.

474

Arrange your workday to include time
for innovating on the job.

475

Choose to patronize places where the music is low.

476

Daily meditation is an opportunity to check in
with the peace inside your mind.

477

Get rid of extra stuff: Give to the needy,
sell, recycle, or dump it.

478

Enrich your time with friends by being attentive,
loving, open, and sympathetic.

479

Listen to the melody of a bird and the
whisper of a breeze.

480

Pause for a few extra seconds before
starting any routine activity.

481

Ask yourself, "What bad thing will happen
if I don't keep moving and doing?
Can I just *be* for a while?"

482

Before you eat, close your eyes, release thoughts,
and give thanks. Notice how this changes
your experience of eating.

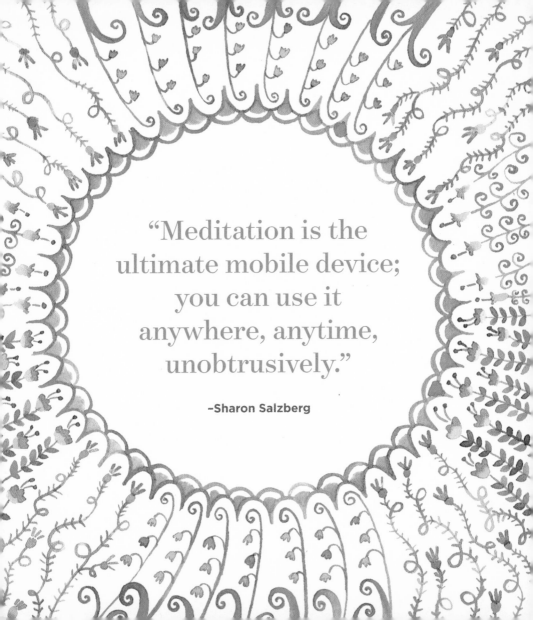

"Meditation is the ultimate mobile device; you can use it anywhere, anytime, unobtrusively."

–Sharon Salzberg

483
Tell your family that you love and appreciate them.

484
Listen closely to the messages in your gut.
There is a genius residing in your core.

485
Take time for people-watching.

486
Think of a clear, flowing brook with fresh water
that gently cleanses and refreshes you
until you feel calm.

487
Stroking pets is therapeutic to both
the human and the pet.

488

Allow your eyes to relax and focus on nothing,
while maintaining a general awareness
of everything. See how this feels compared
to staring at something purposefully.

489

Humans need a break from the psychological
demands of interaction and reaction.

490

Frequent beaches with no concession
stands, vendors, volleyball games, or
even parking lots.

491

Wait to take your turn.

492

Don't hurry to use up food unless it is
nearing its expiration date.

493

Skip Spinning class and take a lazy bike ride outside.

494

Walking across the office to talk
to someone face-to-face can actually
save time and money. Email does not capture
nuance or body language and often leads
to misunderstanding and mistakes.

495

As you cut and arrange flowers, ponder nature
and how she takes her time creating
these beautiful gifts.

496

Make a still life of beautiful objects as
a focus for contemplation.

497

Break into laughter during a heated discussion.

498

Ten minutes before bedtime, do a focused
mindfulness exercise.

499

Become aware of how much downtime you need.

500

Take your time with your personal
grooming routine.

"Most problems,
if you give them enough
time and space,
will eventually wear
themselves out."

–Buddha

501

Hear everyday sounds as "mindfulness bells":
a church bell, a telephone ringtone, a doorbell,
the ding of a new email, etc. When you hear them,
pause, breathe, and reconnect with
the present moment.

502

When facing criticism or a misunderstanding,
take time to pause.

503

Allow 30 to 45 minutes for an evening bath.

504

If you talk about work while you are
on vacation, you are not on vacation.

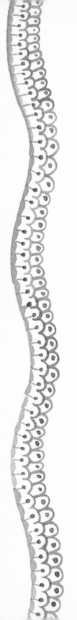

505

Learn basic acupressure and reflexology techniques
that you can use on yourself.

506

Use the oven instead of the microwave.

507

If you stay with the moment, you will have
enough time to do what needs to be done.

508

Release tension with gentle head
and shoulder rolls.

509

Make time to ask for forgiveness
from yourself and others.

510

Take a break from the electric toothbrush
to brush your teeth slowly.

511

Lose the list for a day.

512

Break your work into 30-minute increments.
When you get distracted, note the distraction
but continue to focus on the task at hand.

513

Do a little creative work each day before you
get started on "regular" work.

514

Hang up a "do not disturb" sign up for awhile.

Calm List

Activities to Keep Kids Occupied for Hours

Baking from scratch

Board game day

Building a blanket fort

Creating an obstacle course

Exploring a natural history museum

Picnicking at a state park

Planting a garden

Reading any Harry Potter book

Scavenger hunt

Science experiment

Trip to the zoo

Visiting a living museum

515

Make time for yourself by first
de-cluttering your mind.

516

Try a new slow-cooker recipe.

517

Wait for the passenger door to be unlocked
before you yank on the handle.

518

Appreciate times of idleness, especially
when you are not idle by choice.

519

Indulge in mini-retirements from work:
Take advantage of sabbatical programs,
vacation time, personal days, etc.

520

Take a break by looking out a window
or going outside.

521

Bag your own groceries after
scanning them yourself.

522

Keep something funny on your desk
as a reminder to lighten up.

523
Moments of presence can make
a big difference in your day.

524
Don't try to force yourself to come up
with an idea. It will come when
you least expect it.

525
Slowing down allows you to appreciate ordinary
moments as extraordinary.

526
Let your mind unfurl and your soul unfold.

"Have patience with
all things, but chiefly
have patience
with yourself."

–St. Francis de Sales

527

Learn to grill your meat and vegetables on low.

528

Golf only when you don't have a time limit.

529

Attune yourself to birdsong.

530

Most airports have nondenominational chapels.
On a layover, visit one of these peaceful,
silent places.

531

Once a year, look through all of your old photographs.

532

Don't just do something;
sit there.

533

Let yourself rest.

534

Choose to live like a tree that bears
fruit slowly, for decades.

535

Slowing down can help you move
from autopilot to attention.

536

Let go of the stuff that is not your responsibility
and not your problem.

537

Skip mediocre television shows.

538

Reflect on all the times you opened your mouth and spoke empty words to fill a silence.

539

See life as a journey and appreciate the twists, turns, and bumps in the road.

540

Get joy from waiting for things to happen, like holding a fishing pole for hours.

541

Ask the oldest member of your family to tell you a story about his or her childhood.

Calm List

Ways to Switch Off
Your Autopilot

Breathe slowly and deeply. Figure out where you
feel the breath in your body.

Spend quality time with your pet.

Connect with another person. Get them
to talk about themselves.

Consciously perform a task in slow motion.

Take the time to be kind or compliment others
instead of rushing away.

Go outside and feel the wind, see the sky, and touch a plant.

Listen deeply to another person.

Take in the ambient sounds around you.

Narrate the task you are trying to perform
to stay focused.

Notice your judgments. Switch to
unconditional love.

Think about the stories you tell yourself.

Be an observer of your mind and the restlessness
that often takes place there.

Pay attention to your surroundings
when you drive or walk.

Practice mindfulness.

Sit in stillness: stop moving, stop doing,
stop rehashing, stop planning.

Tune in to your body's feelings and movements.

Be aware of when you can go farther
and when it is time to pull back.

542

When you live at a slower pace, it's easier
to see what is harmful and embrace
what is beneficial.

543

Deliberately bring more patience to
a conversation or a relationship.

544

Think of the core of your being as the center
of a cyclone or tornado. Whatever happens
around that center does not affect it.

545

Wait for a movie to be available for rent.

546

Genuine peace is to be discovered in
every moment. Peace is not a reward
for a lifetime of struggle.

547

Make a weekly dinner plan so you buy
all the ingredients in one shopping trip.

548

Instead of cramming in one more thing,
save it for tomorrow.

549

How would your sense of time change
if you spent a week alone?

550
Sing out loud!

551
If you are always ahead of schedule,
then there is no need to rush.

552
Observe as a butterfly flutters and
then slowly goes on its way.

553
When you wake up, immediately think how
you can give joy to someone today.

554
Remove your watch and ignore clocks
to the best of your ability.

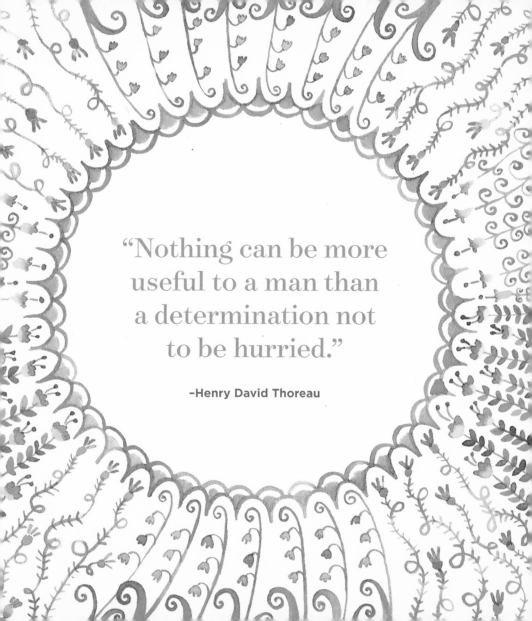

"Nothing can be more
useful to a man than
a determination not
to be hurried."

–Henry David Thoreau

555

Peel an apple or orange in a
single strip, performing the task
slowly and with concentration.

556

Imagine time slowing down so that you are
almost unaware of its passing.

557

History is full of stories of inspirations coming
in idle moments and dreams: Archimedes'
legendary Eureka moment in the bath and
Newton's apple falling from the tree are examples.

558

Experience the present moment
in complete stillness.

559
Eating at a gentle pace gives the stomach time to tell the brain that it is getting full.

560
Giving yourself a break from overworking increases your brainpower and creativity.

561
Before you go to work, reinforce your resolve to stay as calm and relaxed as possible.

562
Drawing and painting are meditative activities.

563
Feel the wind on your face.

564

Pick a place in your home to be your sanctuary.

565

Study the long migrations of caribou,
swallows, leatherback sea turtles, whales,
and wildebeest. These slow journeys
of great accuracy teach us much about enjoying
the road, not just the destination.

566

If you have trouble sleeping, jot down
what is on your mind. Then let it go
until tomorrow.

567

Take the time to give someone directions
if they are lost.

568

Know that the opposite of talking
is waiting and listening.

569

Stop wishing for the toaster, the coffeemaker,
or the microwave to work faster.

570

Walk at half speed.

571

It takes a lot of time to achieve
"instant" success.

572

Sigh with ease.

573

Enjoy the smug satisfaction you feel
when there is a hidden scene after
the movie credits and you waited
till the very end.

574

Relax in a Jacuzzi.

575

Go shopping and tell everyone
you are "just looking."

576

Give up urgency.

577

Allow yoga to give strong emotions
a gentle physical release.

578

Some say that grapes and grape products
relax your blood vessels.

579

Grind your coffee beans with a mortar
and pestle or a hand-driven mill.

580

Make homemade tomato sauce from
the tomatoes in your garden.

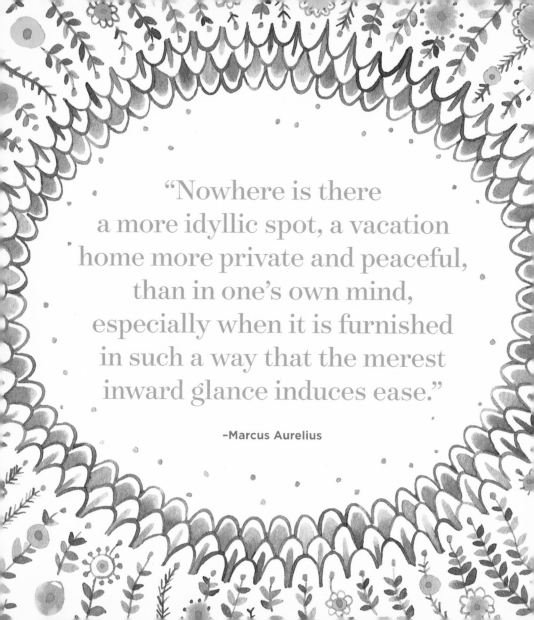

"Nowhere is there a more idyllic spot, a vacation home more private and peaceful, than in one's own mind, especially when it is furnished in such a way that the merest inward glance induces ease."

–Marcus Aurelius

581

When you get to your seat on an airplane,
sit, breathe, and relax.

582

Don't let negative thoughts weigh you down.
Your spirit will feel lighter.

583

A thought can flow like a breaking wave—
curving under and going inside itself,
then disappearing to a place
where it will repeat the cycle.

584

Learn at least one relaxation technique
and practice it often.

585
Do a jigsaw puzzle.

586
Develop a wellness plan.

587
Wait for the paperback version.

588
Spend time with a small child and see
through their eyes.

589
Savor those delicious extra few minutes in bed,
when you should really be on your way to work.

590

Look away from the computer screen.

591

Make time for cuddling.

592

Learning takes time, but every second
is worth it.

593

Choose to enjoy yourself.

594

Seek help from others.
You are not alone.

595

Say a prayer for slowing down.

596

Consider how the magazines you read affect
the way you spend your time and money.

597

Notice that even the loudest sounds are
impermanent, passing away into silence.

598

Wear down your restlessness.

599

An unhurried mind brings the capacity
to make wise choices every day.

Calm List

Ways to Spend Extra Time Outdoors

Boating

Exploring a wilderness area

Hanging out at a swimming pool

Lying in a hammock

Participating in a conservation program

Relaxing in an outdoor café

Strolling the grounds of a large church, college, or university

Taking a parks and recreation course

Visiting a rooftop green space

Walking a path along the water

600

Set up a bird feeder outside your window
and watch the birds come and go.

601

Practice the patient art of origami.

602

Laughter is the best medicine.

603

Slow down at a time when you regularly
speed up, like when getting ready for bed.

604

Take time for spring cleaning.

605

Don't rush to judgment. Try to look at matters
from multiple points of view.

606

Breaking hurried patterns is a step
toward intentional living.

607

If you must buy take-out food,
find a peaceful place to enjoy your meal.

608

After you return from travel, try to take
an extra day off to ease back into life.

609

Stop trying to change people. You will
save so much time and energy.

610

Start the day with meditation, exercise,
a leisurely breakfast, and a shower.

611

Cook dinner with your partner as a form
of entertainment and communion.

612

Go out without a plan. Let serendipity
and coincidence be your guides.

613

Doodle. Unleash your creativity
for your own private pleasure.

614

When you feel stressed, take time out
for your favorite relaxation activity.

615

Lounge.

616

Sit in a café and don't talk to anyone.

617

Banish the terms "should" and "have to."

"There is no hurry.
We shall get there
some day."

–A. A. Milne,
The House at Pooh Corner

618

Idleness is not just an indulgence or vice,
it is indispensable to the brain.

619

Search for the hidden gems in thrift shops.

620

When you are moving through life too fast,
you inevitably eat fast, which creates digestive upset.

621

Swim.

622

Shave with a manual razor rather
than an electric shaver.

623

Before you go to sleep, be aware of the
different regions of your body and allow
yourself to experience how each part feels,
without trying to change anything.

624

Be relaxed and flexible (yin) while maintaining
a sense of focus and purpose (yang).

625

Enjoy a "lived-in" home. Who are you
trying to impress, anyway?

626

Listen to some cool jazz.

627

While you are waiting, look around
for something beautiful.

628

Think deeply.

629

Enjoy eating sweets occasionally.

630

Self-discipline is about exerting boundaries,
control, and limits on oneself in order
to make positive changes.

631
When you feel yourself getting angry,
breathe in and out for at least the count of 10.

632
Put a note in a bottle and send it
down a waterway.

633
Remember a setting you loved.
Go there in your mind and linger.

634
Collect items to bury in a time capsule.

635
Pressing a flower is a slow pleasure.

636
Stretch—and feel the tension flow out of you.

637
Life is easier when it is simple.

638
Mow the lawn less frequently.

639
Listen with no expectation, interpretation, preconception, or prejudice.

640
Focusing your mind on one object reduces the number of signals to your brain, so you can settle into a deeply relaxed yet highly alert state.

Remember to Practice Breathing

Alternate Nostril Breathing

Press your right thumb to the side of your right nostril.
Inhale through your left nostril for 8 counts.
Then shut both nostrils, keeping your right thumb in place
and placing your right index finger on the left nostril.
Hold for as long as you feel comfortable. Then let go
of the right side, exhaling. Repeat, inhaling on
the right side. Alternate 10 times.

Anytime Deep Breathing

Take deep slow breaths while on the phone, in the car,
or waiting for just about anything.

Counting Breaths for Focus

Inhale and count "one," then exhale and count "two."
Count from 1 to 10 and then start again.

Slow Breathing

Once a day, sit or lie down on the floor and stretch.
Feel the breath moving in your body. When you
recognize a deep, slow breath, you can say "deep"
as you breathe in and "slow" as you breathe out.
Do this for 5 to 10 minutes.

Three-Part Breathing

Inhale through your nose for 4 counts, hold for 16,
then exhale through your nose for 8. A beginner
might start with 1 count, hold for 4, exhale for 2.
Do 3 sets.

Ujjayi (Victorious) Breathing*

Inhale through your nose, gently constricting
the back of your throat. Pause at the top of the breath.
Then exhale into your closed mouth. Your breath
should sound like Darth Vader. Continue with
your mouth closed. Do this for 10 cycles.

* Used in Taoist and yoga practices.

641

Allot double the time for projects.

642

Picnic beside a babbling brook.

643

Practice qigong, a system of exercise
integrating physical postures,
breathing techniques, focused attention,
and mindful intent.

644

Take time to think before you act.

645

Practice patience.

646

Wait to buy an outfit until it goes on sale.

647

Empty time is not a vacuum to be filled.

648

Your breath will tell you if you are
going too quickly, too slowly, or if you are
moving at just the right speed.

649

Plant a garden.

650

When you are sick, your body is
telling you to take a break.

651

Sit in a chair, close your eyes, and just relax.

652

Giving up an addictive substance,
such as alcohol or sugar,
will empower you.

653

Think of the brief silence that occurs
when driving under an overpass during
a raging thunderstorm.

654

When you see an animal trying to cross
the road, slow down and offer it safe passage.

655

Use free evenings to pursue new interests.

656

Rather than judging a moment,
accept it for what it is.

657

Yoga can help reduce stress, lower blood pressure,
and improve heart function.

658

Take the time to appreciate a family keepsake
that has been passed down through the years.

659

Give up on the book you are reading
if you are not enjoying it.

660

Eat a piece of bread so slowly that you can
feel the sun, soil, and rain that supported
the wheat as it grew.

661

Be open and receptive to whatever comes into
your field of awareness. Let it all come and go.
Watch in stillness.

"Sitting quietly,
doing nothing,
Spring comes,
and the grass grows
by itself."

–Zen proverb

662

Take your time. It is *your* time, and it is
up to you what you do with it.

663

Be silent for a whole day.

664

If you are feeling blue, don't try to figure out
what is wrong. Rather, let your mind settle
and clear as best you can, and let go.

665

Prepare for sleep by thinking calm thoughts.

666

Leave time for small, sacred rituals in your life.

667

Do not needlessly occupy your mind.
Just be.

668

Take five minutes in the morning
to plan your day.

669

Mail an envelope to a fake address on the other
side of the globe. See how long it takes to travel
around the world and come back to you.

670
Whenever you hear the quiet voice of intuition,
pay attention to its advice.

671
When you feel impatient, try putting the
other person's comfort and convenience first.
Build your relationships with others this way.

672
Go on a leisurely outing with
family or friends.

673
Bake pies with whatever fruit is in season.

674

Watch a passing scene. Be an observer, forming no judgment.

675

Stroll down a city street during Christmas season and admire the department store windows decked out for the holidays.

676

Try tantra, a slower, more mental approach to sexual encounters, which is based on enjoying powerful mind-body connections with your partner and increased intimacy.

"Sometimes I think there
are only two instructions
we need to follow to develop
and deepen our spiritual life:
slow down and let go."

–Oriah Mountain Dreamer

677
Pause to be grateful before each meal.

678
Climb a tree.

679
Let go of your expectations of others.

680
If you don't like a particular holiday,
bow out. Go camping instead.

681
Build a house of cards.

682

Create a phrase or a gesture that you can use
to instantly ground yourself.
Do this whenever you feel rattled.

683

Bring cut flowers inside to enjoy.

684

Listen to the small sounds of your home
that make you feel at ease.

685

Have a long conversation with
someone you care about.

686

Be limacine, like a slug, or testudinate,
like a turtle.

687

Take breaks for short meditations, affirmations,
and offerings of gratitude.

688

Light a candle.

689

Hug your pet.

690

Sometimes the best thing to do is not think,
not wonder, not imagine—just breathe.

691

Arrange your books or old records in
alphabetical order or by genre. Remember what
you love about each one as you organize.

692

Imagine an ant or worm crawling
through the grass.

693

Hang out with friends, with no
mobile devices allowed!

Slow Synonyms

ambling	idle	shuffling
cautious	languid	slack
circumspect	languorous	snaillike
crawling	leisurely	strolling
creeping	lingering	tarrying
dallying	lollygagging	tentative
dawdling	moderate	toddling
deliberate	poking	tortoiselike
eased	poky	tottering
easy	relaxed	turtlelike
easy-paced	sauntering	unhurried
gentle	savoring	waddling

694

Relaxation pose: Lie down and let your
legs and arms relax and flop out naturally.
Close your eyes and relax your facial muscles.
Melt into the earth. Focus on your breath
going in and out wherever you feel it strongest.
Stay in this position for 5 to 20 minutes.

695

Resist your urge to grab another snack
or cup of coffee. Focus on what you are doing.
Let go of both the urge and restlessness.

696

Let your mind run like a dog
on an empty stretch of beach.

697

Ride a slow train and watch the world go by.

698

Try to do one errand at a time.

699

Learn to accept inaction.

700

Try to plan meals so you can focus on
your family instead of the food.

701

On snow days, let go of your worries
about missing work and enjoy the snow.

702
Sink into a favorite chair and savor
some silence.

703
Stop at enough.

704
Why rehearse future conversations that may
never actually happen? Be here now.

705
When you feel peaceful, you can
quiet others' storms.

706
Reject the mind-set of "do more,
achieve more, acquire more."

707
Chop your own wood.

708
Bake homemade bread.

709
Don't binge-watch television shows.
Stretch out the enjoyment.

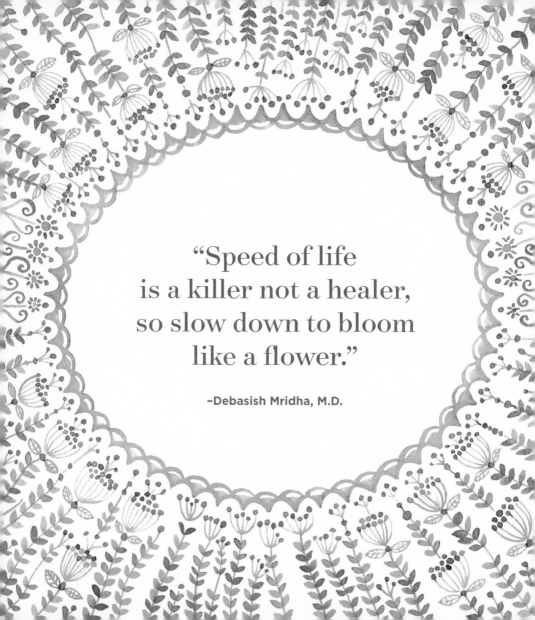

"Speed of life
is a killer not a healer,
so slow down to bloom
like a flower."

–Debasish Mridha, M.D.

710

Cook a meal from scratch.

711

Sitting still is a way of falling in love
with the world and everything in it.

712

Leave your shoes at the front door.
Leave your troubles with the shoes.

713

Constantly doing is a habit. You can also
develop the opposite habit of just being.

714
Do not fear silence.

715
Search slowly for very smooth stones.

716
Make midcourse corrections during the day.
Simply closing your eyes
and breathing deeply will help.

717
Visit a zoo, where the pace of an animal's life
is on display.

718

Treat your home as a sanctuary.

719

A short period of quiet inspiration in the morning
will anchor the rest of your day.

720

Close your eyes and turn your attention inward.
This is your inner sanctuary of peace and stillness.

721

Walk around a usually hectic business district
on a quiet weekend.

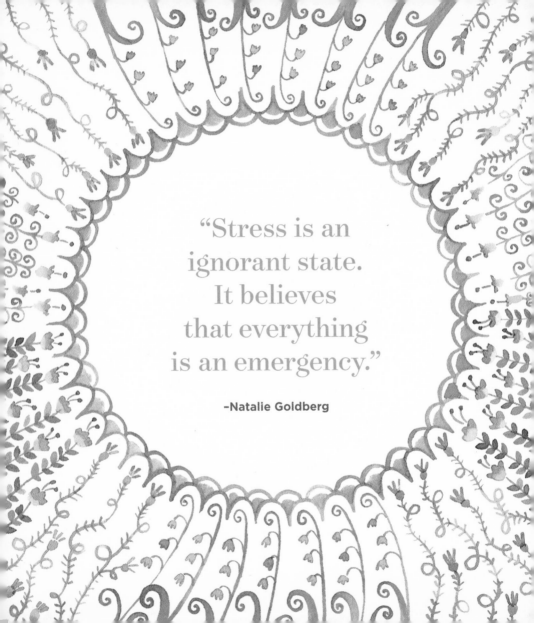

"Stress is an
ignorant state.
It believes
that everything
is an emergency."

–Natalie Goldberg

722

Practice gratitude.

723

In the spring, put on boots and tramp
through wet fields and woods to remind
yourself of all the things that were buried
or forgotten during winter.

724

Learn to do calligraphy.

725

Get your news from a slower source than
a ticker sliding across the TV screen.

726

Think of yourself as a pebble falling through clear water. Then let your mind and body come to repose, like the pebble resting in the sand.

727

Take a little longer than usual to reply.

728

Instead of spinning best- and worst-case scenarios, just breathe and let strong emotions dissipate.

729

Thought is just thought.
It is not compelling or urgent.

730

Take 30 days to read your monthly magazine.

731

Take control of the information overload.
What do you really want to read,
reply to, or watch on TV?

732

Think of the slow driver in front of you
as protecting you from driving too fast.

733

Wait for the tide by the shore.

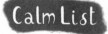
Calm List

Productive Ways to Slow Down at Work

Block Out Quiet Time
Schedule time on your calendar for tasks that require long periods of concentration.

Brainstorm
Take time to generate new ideas and forge projects of your own design.

Change Your Workspace
Move to an area where you will be better able to think. A change of scene can provide fresh insights.

Get Organized
An hour of planning at the start of a major project will save weeks later in the process.

Go Out for Lunch
Socializing with colleagues strengthens workplace relationships, which helps you get things done.

Make a To-Do List
Review this list every morning and
make a plan for the day.

Take Breaks
You will be more productive when
you get back.

Vary Your Routine
Any change will temporarily slow
you down. The reward is having more time
to process and absorb information,
improving your work performance.

Work Off-Site
Doing your job at home or in a coffeehouse
may give you a fresh perspective.

Work Shorter Hours
Some studies show that getting more done
at work won't make you as happy as simply
working less. Taking time for your hobbies
and exercise will increase the quality of
the time you spend on work.

734

The more you pay attention to what
is happening around you,
the slower time seems to move.

735

Don't buy that book until you have
the time to read it.

736

Make a meal for a friend who is
going through a hard time.

737

Take a play break in a busy workday.

738

Free time can enable your mind
to creatively rearrange itself.

739

Massage your face and scalp,
where much tension is held.

740

Look under a large stone when you are
walking in the forest. You will discover
a new world beneath it.

741

Look for some small thing that can restore
your soul, stimulate your thinking, and fill you
with a gratitude for being here.

742
Let the sunlight wake you in the morning.

743
Pack your own lunch.

744
Pay attention to shadows.

745
Let another driver have that parking spot.

746
When confronted by an angry person,
simply observe his or her unhappiness
and breathe in.

"Take rest; a field that has rested gives a bountiful crop."

–Ovid

747

Do one thing at a time.

748

The slow-down philosophy can be
summed up in a word: "balance."
It is seeking to live at the right speed—
not too fast and not too slow.

749

Read about Zen.

750

Try to crack a code.

751

Watch the trees, flowers, and plants stand tall
when they see the sun.

752

Go on a scavenger hunt in the forest.
Seek hard-to-find items
and enjoy the search.

753

Avoid the natural urge to speed up.

754

Sit on a porch or park bench by yourself.

755

Get your work done and then focus
on other things.

756

Block out unplanned time in your schedule.
Then when the moment arrives, get up
and do something spontaneous.

757

Leave some things unsaid.

758

Look up into the night sky
and ponder its mysteries.

759
Your productivity increases
when you slow down.

760
Stress cannot run your life if you don't
cultivate its existence.

761
Every cup of coffee is an excuse to be present
in the moment.

762
Walk slowly on crunchy snow or autumn leaves,
attending to the crackle of each step.

Board Games to Savor

Agricola

Game of Thrones

Jenga

Life

Monopoly

Risk

Roads & Boats

Scrabble

Sequence

Talisman

Through the Ages

Ticket to Ride

Trajan

763

Doing something else while you're eating takes away from tasting and fully enjoying the food.

764

Open a book at random and read for a short while.

765

Take the time to recycle.

766

Sink into your couch.

767

Wade through puddles
during a rainstorm.

768

Read gravestones. Stories are there
to be discovered.

769

Stop sprinting through your day.
What race are you trying to win?

770

Take a time-out.

771

The best investment of your limited time
on Earth is to spend it with people you love.

772

Don't buy Christmas presents before Halloween
or decorate before Thanksgiving.

773

Slowing down means you control
the rhythms of your own life.

774

Rediscover childhood pleasures,
such as blowing bubbles, making
paper dolls, or coloring.

775

Taking a less-is-more approach to hobbies
can ease the pressure to fit them in.

776

Drive less, walk more.

777

Every day, when you return home
from work, rejoice.

778

Let an idea simmer in the back of your mind.

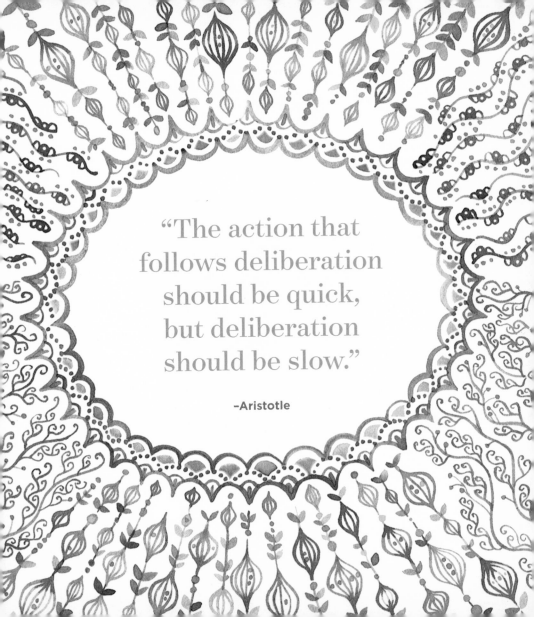

"The action that
follows deliberation
should be quick,
but deliberation
should be slow."

–Aristotle

779

You do not need to get more things done faster;
you need to do fewer things better.

780

Walk barefoot outside.

781

See a long airplane flight as a retreat in the sky.

782

Consider quitting a committee
or club if you are overextended.

783

Connect body, breath, and beauty.

784

Before you make an online purchase,
put the item in your shopping cart and see
if you remember it's there a week later.

785

In feng shui, burning a yellow candle
promotes calm.

786

Yawn as often as you feel like it.

Alternatives to Fast Machines

Being Creative
Reading, writing, or drawing on paper
is more fulfilling than watching television
or surfing the Internet.

Climbing Stairs
In buildings with elevators and escalators,
take the stairs. These little bursts of exercise
can energize your day.

Eschewing the Dishwasher
Skipping the dishwasher means less noise and
not having to empty it later.

Going to the Library
Use this community resource instead of ordering
books online or downloading e-books.

Rowing a Boat
Paddling out on the water is more fun and enriching
than using a rowing machine in a gym.

Shopping in Brick-and-Mortar Stores
Returning an online purchase may cost you
both time and postage.

Talking Face-to-Face
Communicating with a loved one in person offers
a stronger personal connection than talking
by telephone, email, or text message.

Using a Manual Lawn Mower
Slow mowing allows time to meditate and commune with
nature. Plus it's good exercise and is kinder to the environment.

Walking or Biking to Work
Get fresh air and exercise instead of battling traffic
or crowds on public transportation.

Washing Clothes by Hand
Letting them air-dry can lengthen the life of the clothes.

787

Draw a still life.

788

Ask your partner for a slow dance
after a fast day.

789

An outward smile can enhance
your inner peace.

790

Break down a large or unfamiliar task
into smaller, more manageable parts.

791

Performing a task in a slow manner
often yields better results.

792

Take the time to bury your face
in a lilac bush.

793

Removing some items from your bucket list
creates space for the little things
that bring happiness.

794

Begin an activity with one gentle inhalation
and a calm exhalation, no matter
what that activity is.

"You just have to keep
driving down the road.
It's going to bend and curve
and you'll speed up
and slow down, but the
road keeps going."

–Ellen DeGeneres

795

When you see yourself getting angry,
observe how your mind is speeding up.
Try to step back rather than react.

796

Leave work at work.

797

Take time to reflect, set priorities,
and listen.

798

Sit on the steps on summer evenings
and watch the lightning bugs.

799
Do deep-breathing exercises before
giving a presentation.

800
Learning to trust life is like learning to swim.
First you flail, convinced you will drown.
Then you notice that if you calm down,
you can tread water. And when you let go
and relax, you realize that the water was there
to support you all along.

801
Give yourself permission to abandon
any personal project midway.

802

Notice the color of the sky.

803

Take time each day to hunt for beauty.

804

Add massage to lovemaking.

805

If an angry driver wants to zoom past you,
let him. You will have a calm heart,
while that driver will still be angry.

806

When it is hard to start a project or task,
take one small step.

807

Enjoy a shoeshine.

808

Choose restaurants that have a calming,
nourishing atmosphere.

809

Stare out a window.

810

Shop less and take back those hours.

811

Pay attention to sound, smell,
taste, and touch.

812

Go to a movie, sit in the dark,
and be transported.

813

Stand back and look at life as a whole.
This is when inspiration strikes.

814

To simplify your life, create routines for sleep,
housework, grocery shopping, and meals.

815

In your spiritual life, the greatest changes
are made slowly and gradually.

816

Not asking for the answer will give you time
to ponder the question.

817

Practice yoga. It increases the types of prana
(life energy force) that calm, soothe,
and ground you.

"There must be
quite a few things
a hot bath won't cure,
but I don't know
many of them."

–Sylvia Plath,
The Bell Jar

818

Smile and slow down.

819

Learn to keep your cool by remaining
slow inside.

820

Making lists saves time and worry.

821

Teach your kids the joy of solitude. They will
carry this gift throughout their lives.

822
Accept change.

823
Expecting a long wait? Come up with things you can do in a span of 10 to 30 minutes.

824
About every 90 to 120 minutes, we experience an "ultradian dip" when energy drops. After 90 to 120 minutes of focused attention, honor your ultradian rhythms and take a 20-minute break.

825

Think about the things you have bought
on impulse. Did you really use these items?

826

Apply a brake to your brain.

827

When you feel a spontaneous rush of love
or compassion, don't hurry on to the next moment.
Allow the feeling to deepen.

828

Why waste energy trying to impress others?
Choose to be yourself.

829

Recognize that your "wasted day"
was actually the break you needed.

830

In a museum or gallery, spend time
with the painting that draws you in instead
of the painting everyone goes there to see.

831

Put off procrastination.

832

As you take in the natural world,
let nature touch you.

Calm List

Things You Cannot Speed Up

Baking a cake

Brain synapses

Caterpillars

Elevators

Evolution

Falling in love

Formation of stalagmites and stalactites

Glaciers

Movement of the planets, stars, sun, and moon

Nerve impulses

Snails

Weather

833

Sometimes the earliest hours are best
for doing nothing.

834

Make time to volunteer.

835

Before you do something that could
cause a problem, stop. Imagine the possible
outcomes of your action and make a choice.

836

Take a few moments to keep your contacts list
up-to-date. It will save you time later.

837

Have you ever eaten on autopilot and then
still felt hungry? Eat mindfully.

838

If you do not have enough time for exercise,
include it in daily activities. Take the stairs
or walk a block farther to get your lunch.

839

Take a staycation.

840

A pause is the gift of time—the time
to become calm and centered.

841
Wait out a sudden downpour.

842
Does being busy make you happier?

843
When trying out a new hobby,
don't look for a quick result.

844
Imagine a hive surrounded by honeybees,
each bee representing a niggling problem of yours.
Visualize the bees disappearing one at a time into
the hive—then notice how your mind quiets.

845
Look forward to special occasions,
enjoy the planning process, and then be sure
to enjoy the moment when the event arrives.

846
Working from home is sometimes more efficient,
allowing for fewer interruptions.

847
Give yourself permission to get
thoroughly and happily lost.

848
Don't leave a sporting event early just to
get ahead of traffic. Cutting the game short
detracts from the experience.

"There's never enough time to do all the nothing you want."

–Bill Watterson,
"Calvin and Hobbes"

849

Eat dinner with your family every night.

850

Practice layered listening:
Notice the most obvious sounds,
and then the next layer down, etc.

851

Get lost in the sounds of a storm.

852

You will drive more safely if you leave
15 minutes early to get to an appointment.

853

Pay attention to the gap between the
in-breath and the out-breath.

854

It can be energizing to share yourself
with others.

855

Join the slow food movement:
Replace processed foods with whole foods;
eat organic, locally grown food;
and cook and eat slowly.

856

Count turtles to go to sleep.

857

Intentionally stand in the longest line
at the grocery store. Breathe slowly
and focus on your patience level.

858

Whittle or sculpt something.

859

Carry a small object that reminds you
to stay calm.

860

When you model calm behavior,
people around you—including children—
will also be calmer.

861

Watch the waves at the beach.

862

Teach yourself to do things without
watching the clock.

863

Lie down on a couch by a sunny window.

Calm List

Activities to Do at a Slower Pace

Breathing
Inhaling and exhaling more slowly and deeply
helps reduce anxiety, depression, and stress.

Eating
You will consume fewer calories, enjoy your food,
and have better digestion if you eat more slowly.

Media Ingestion
Take a break from binge-watching.
Watch a half hour or an hour here and there,
then let yourself absorb what you've seen.

Reading
Slow reading can improve concentration
and deepen comprehension.

Talking
Fast talking is easy to ignore. If you speak slower, you will take more care with your words. Others will hear you better and listen more closely.

Thinking
Making space between thoughts will help your mind become calmer.

Waking Up
Stretch, smile, and set your intentions for the day. Start off on the right foot.

Walking
You'll enjoy nature more, and you'll probably walk more properly (heel-to-toe roll).

Weight Lifting
Lowering the weight is just as important as lifting it. You'll benefit on the way up and on the way down.

864

Remember that there is silence
under the chaos.

865

Don't be productive all the time.

866

Chat with random people as you run errands.
We all need face-to-face interaction.

867

It is possible to do things quickly
while maintaining a slow frame of mind.

868

Turning a computer all the way off lets you
experience a time without the hum
of electronics.

869

When you play beautiful music,
be mindful of each note.

870

Inhale deeply. Silently count "one."
Exhale completely. Count "two."
Continue breathing and counting up
to ten, then backward to one.

871

What kind of nothing makes you happiest?

872

Think of cats, asleep much of the time
yet acutely aware of what is going on
around them. The cat is simply being itself
wholeheartedly. It is in the present moment,
open to whatever occurs.

873

Instead of doing everything, do the things
that are most important to you.

874

View completing an errand as equally
important as completing a major project.
Every mundane detail is part of your
time on Earth.

875
Don't try to be the first to finish a test, quiz, or project. Enjoy the learning journey.

876
Slow-eat chocolate or caramels.

877
Schedule solo getaways.

878
Cook homemade macaroni and cheese.

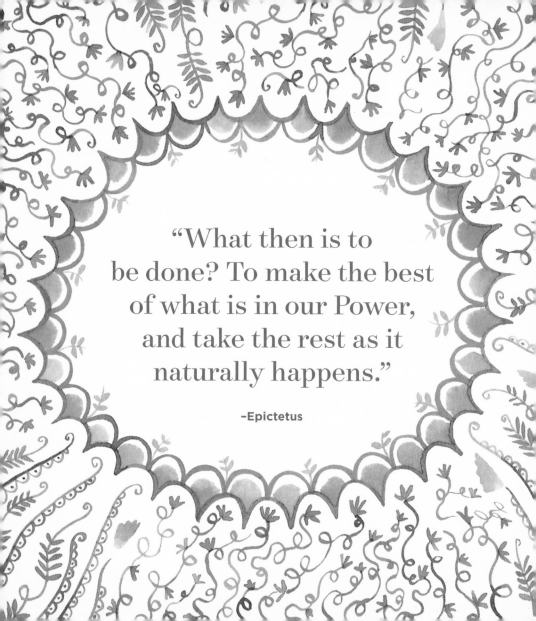

"What then is to be done? To make the best of what is in our Power, and take the rest as it naturally happens."

–Epictetus

879

To see the mind is to free the mind.

880

Visualize yourself rowing a boat toward
an island. Feel each pull of the oars
and let your breath grow slower and longer.
Imagine yourself arriving at the shore.

881

Make greeting cards for family and friends.

882

Pausing means expanding into the moment
instead of feeling cramped by it.

883

Take your time choosing your meal
at a restaurant.

884

Relax your hands while driving.

885

Consider waking up a little earlier to
make time for something you enjoy.

886

Learn about rocks and minerals—
they have been here longer than we have
and will be here after we depart.

887
Take time to eat before you go grocery shopping.

888
Start taking care of yourself now.
Don't wait for life to calm down.

889
If you do not want to be interrupted,
do not answer the phone, a text message,
or the doorbell.

890
Work on a farm to become more intimately
acquainted with nature's rhythms.

891

Notice the sights when you drive.

892

Feel the sun on your skin.

893

Kick off your shoes.

894

Think about other people's feelings first.

895

Find time to lend a hand, an ear, a moment.

Time-Consuming Art Projects

Coloring

Giant murals

Handmade jewelry

Homemade paper

Mandalas

Matchstick art

Painting with oil on canvas

Quilting

Sculptures made from metal, wood, or found objects

Simple, structured pattern drawings called tangles

Stained glass

Woodcarving

896

Stay engaged with others in a wakeful
and meaningful way.

897

Look through a microscope
or binoculars to contemplate the small,
the minute, and the faraway.

898

Allow yourself to decompress
after a busy workday.

899

Smell every single rose along your path.

900

Sit quietly with a blank canvas or notebook.
Wait until you are moved to act, then paint
or write, guided by your soul.

901

Not saying anything when you have nothing
to say will always prove wise.

902

Is it true that your life cannot be trivial
or meaningless if you are always busy
and in demand?

903

Cultivate your own produce and herbs.

904
Make time to daydream.

905
If you buy a magazine, read as many
of the articles as you can.

906
Do abdominal crunches slowly
for maximum impact.

907
Watch the flames in your fireplace
until they flicker away.

908
Why hurry? You might be rushing past
all the good things in life.

909
Lie in a drifting boat and look at the sky,
the clouds, the treetops.

910
Be soft-spoken. Loud speech
is usually hurried speech.

911
Wait until the bugs are ironed out
before you try a new gadget.

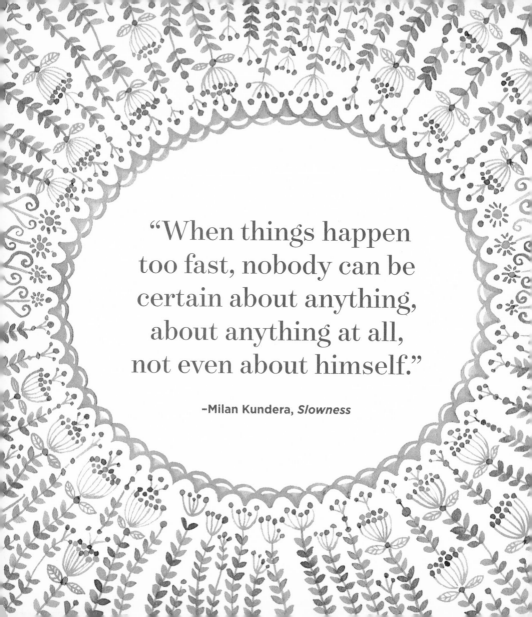

"When things happen too fast, nobody can be certain about anything, about anything at all, not even about himself."

–Milan Kundera, *Slowness*

912

Take a bus instead of an airplane so you can appreciate the distance and the scenery.

913

Go to brunch—the most unhurried of all meals.

914

Are you stretching your work to fill longer hours because all around you others are too?

915

Instead of getting angry about everyday frustrations, accept these situations with humor and serenity.

916

Go easy on yourself when you cannot
make something happen.

917

Precise attention creates clarity.

918

Use a blank TV screen for visualization—
project your dreams onto it.

919

Savor the silent moments before a kiss.

920
Rise slowly from your chair after a good meal.

921
A simpler life will allow you to make
fewer decisions.

922
You have the right to determine
your own tempo.

923
You can retreat to the stillness and sanctuary
within you at any time.

924

Go fast to get someplace, then return slowly.
Do you see the difference?

925

Make up and tell stories to children—a lost art.

926

Rhythmic breathing can calm emotions
and nerves.

927

Wrap up existing commitments
and exercise care in taking on new ones.

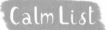
Calm List

Things to Do the Old-Fashioned Way

Hang a paper calendar on your wall.

Keep a journal.

Keep a physical address book.

Listen to the nuances of music on a vinyl record.

Make homemade ice cream.

Make real mashed potatoes.

Pop popcorn on the stove or in the fireplace.

Print out photographs for a photo album.

Read paper books.

Snail mail invitations and greeting cards.

Take pictures with a real camera instead of your smartphone.

928
Learn to say things calmly.

929
Set aside a day a month for a beauty
or spa treatment.

930
Let your ear be a door, allowing sound to enter
but not engaging with the sound.

931
Adequate pacing means not doing
too much at one time.

932

Aim to do everything smoothly
and gracefully.

933

Do not to talk for a few minutes
after a movie ends.

934

Consider the long-term impact
of every choice you make.

935

Relax the rules you set for yourself.

936

Give away little bits of your time without
wishing for anything in return.

937

The company of a friendly canine can
have a powerfully calming effect.

938

Before you go to sleep, make a list of the
little things that make you happy.

939

Eat breakfast slowly.

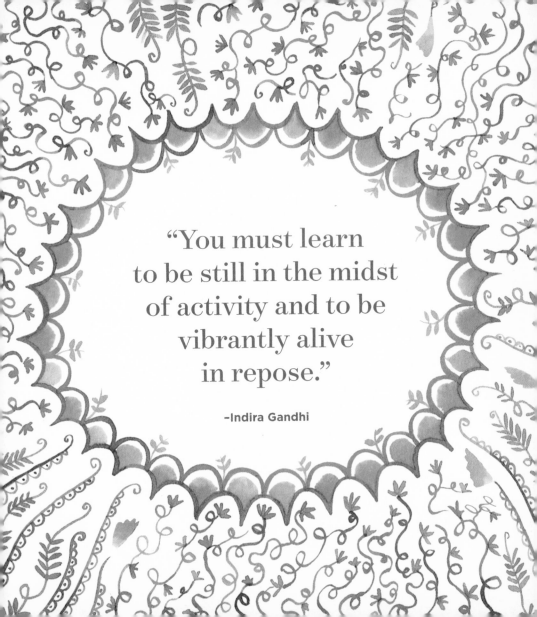

"You must learn
to be still in the midst
of activity and to be
vibrantly alive
in repose."

–Indira Gandhi

940

Spend some time creating, constructing,
or renovating something.

941

Don't hurry your pet to do something.
Animals have a different concept of time
than humans do.

942

Seek out quiet places: a chapel, an art museum,
a library reading room, a botanical garden,
a planetarium, a terrace.

943

Appreciate the heat and humidity for the slowness
it introduces into summer life.

944

Visit a farmers market.

945

Forcing the mind to settle will only stir it up.
Accept your thoughts as they are.

946

Take your time finding art for your home.
Look for pieces (at any price point)
that really speak to you.

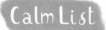
Calm List

What to Do When You Are Forced to Slow Down

Commuting
You cannot control traffic or transportation delays.
Try meditating during this time instead of stressing.

Helping Someone in Need
If you are helping a family member in a
difficult situation, reflect on how good it feels
to be there for someone you care about.

Illness or Injury
When you are sick, injured, or caring for others,
reflect on the benefits of health. Think about
what you want to do with your energy when you
(or the person you are caring for) feels better.

Kids Leaving the Nest
You may think you are ready for this, but you
are not. Take the time to be with your feelings.

Moving

Savor the packing and unpacking. Your home will
only be new for a short while, so enjoy!

Pregnancy

Someone new needs you. Feed the baby and yourself
a lot of quiet and calm as you prepare for the big event.

Processing Grief

If you make yourself too busy to deal with grief,
it will resurface later. Linger over the good memories
and the sadness.

Retirement

Slow down your wake-up routine,
stretch out your exercise, travel leisurely,
take the time to learn new things, and avoid
rushing into new commitments.

School or Job Change

Your judging mind will launch into
comparisons. Allow yourself time to adjust
to the new environment and people.

947

Dally in a doughnut shop.

948

People-watch.

949

Live like you are retired now.

950

Embrace minimalism and you will have time
for the things you've always wanted to do.

951

Go for a hike when the fall foliage is at its peak.

952

Adopt a wait-and-see attitude.

953

Dawdle in the present tense.

954

Who says there is a "right" and "wrong" way
to do everything?

955

An unhurried mind is alert, calm,
and ready for anything.

956

Writing about an event is like experiencing it
in slow motion.

957

Take a mental holiday.

958

Press your tongue against the roof
of your mouth for a few seconds and then relax.
Relaxing the tongue relaxes you.

959

Go on a road trip with someone capable
of handling long stretches of silence.

960

Imagine your life without rushing from
A to B and then to Z.

961

Spend an evening alone, indulging in your
favorite TV shows.

962

Take notes on life.

963

Watch a comedy.

"Drink your tea slowly and reverently, as if it is the axis on which the whole Earth revolves."

–Thich Nhat Hanh

964

When traveling, accept that there is
nothing you can do to get to your
destination faster.

965

Do not take phone calls during family meals.

966

Appreciate time-consuming work done
by you and others.

967

Imagine what it would be like
to always have time to spare, time to breathe,
time to experience, and time to be.

968

Read complete news stories instead of only
the headlines. Appreciate how much time
it took for those stories to be written.

969

Take the whole day off before a holiday.

970

Gaze out the window on a train or airplane.

971

Creating a work of art is a life-affirming process.

972

Trust in life's flow. Sit back and accept
whatever happens.

973

Imagine your mental garbage being carted away
with your real garbage each week.

974

Don't rush to get over a bad mood.

975

Find a quiet refuge outdoors where you can
gather yourself and become peaceful.

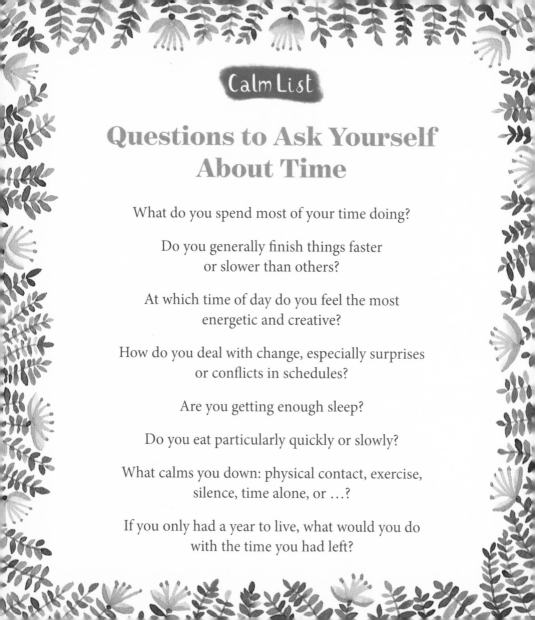

Calm List

Questions to Ask Yourself About Time

What do you spend most of your time doing?

Do you generally finish things faster or slower than others?

At which time of day do you feel the most energetic and creative?

How do you deal with change, especially surprises or conflicts in schedules?

Are you getting enough sleep?

Do you eat particularly quickly or slowly?

What calms you down: physical contact, exercise, silence, time alone, or …?

If you only had a year to live, what would you do with the time you had left?

976

Roll down a grassy bank like you did
when you were a child.

977

Use driving time as a chance to breathe
and reflect without radio or
telephone interruptions.

978

Watch the movie *Big Night*, which shows the art
and pleasure of slow cooking and serving.

979

It's possible to work smarter, not harder.

980

Going into a deep focus (the "zone")
helps you feel calm.

981

Read poetry aloud.

982

Some things cannot or should not be sped up.

983

After meals, give yourself some
quiet time for digestion.

984

Stop checking the forecast.
Accept the weather as it comes.

985
Break the endless cycle of striving for more
by wanting less.

986
Put a problem on the back burner.
Your subconscious may find an answer
while you are doing other things.

987
When you breathe a sigh of relief,
it is your body's way of smiling.

988
Try walking meditation: Break your steps
into slow, mindful movements and breathe,
counting your breaths as you walk.

"A good traveler
has no fixed plans
and is not intent
upon arriving."

–Lao-tzu

989

Kiss the Earth with your feet.

990

Try to telecommute. Gaining free time may be worth a lot more than career "advancement."

991

Breathe out a long *ahhh*.

992

Cook meals with love and creativity.

993

Allow yourself some time off.

994

At the end of the day, look for the stillness
that underlies everything.

995

Consciously do things more slowly
than usual.

996

Always appreciate the time another
person gives to you.

997

Practice letting go and you will
cultivate inner peace.

998
Learn the names of trees, flowers,
and plants in your yard.

999
Make your own list of slow activities.

1,000
If possible, do at least one thing from
your list or this book every week
or every day.

1,001
As you slow down, wisdom will surface
and provide you with needed answers.

Acknowledgments

Thank you to my editor, the fabulous Robin Terry Brown, who is the type of editor I wished for since I started publishing in 1984. Sincere appreciation also goes to Tom Miller, my literary agent. I am very grateful to both for the opportunity to write this book, which is something I have wanted to do for decades.

And many thanks to the very talented Francesca Springolo for her beautiful illustrations. —BaK

About the Author

Barbara Ann Kipfer is a master listmaker and the author of more than 70 books and calendars, including the bestseller *14,000 Things to Be Happy About* (with more than a million copies in print) and *1,001 Ways to Live Wild*. She writes thesauri and dictionaries, trivia and question books, archaeology reference, and happiness- and spiritually-themed books. A professional lexicographer, she holds Ph.D.'s in linguistics, archaeology, and Buddhist studies. Find out more about Kipfer at thingstobe happyabout.com.

Find the Extraordinary in the Ordinary

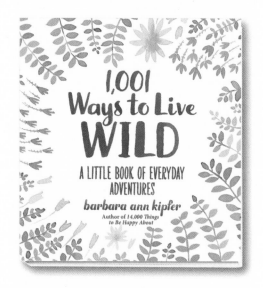

Add a little adventure and whimsy to your life with this irresistible book of inspiration. Discover easy ways to try new things, stay curious, and live life with courage.